MW00908415

IN OUR DUFFEL BAGS

Surviving the Vietnam Era

RICHARD C. GESCHKE

AND

ROBERT A. TOTO

iUniverse, Inc.
Bloomington

In Our Duffel Bags
Surviving the Vietnam Era

iUniverse books may be ordered through booksellers or by contacting:

iUniverse
1663 Liberty Drive
Bloomington, IN 47403
www.iuniverse.com
1-800-Authors (1-800-288-4677)

ISBN: 978-1-4620-2354-7 (sc)
ISBN: 978-1-4620-2353-0 (e)
ISBN: 978-1-4620-2355-4 (dj)

Library of Congress Control Number: 2011908884

Printed in the United States of America

iUniverse rev. date: 7/21/2011

To all US military veterans

CONTENTS

PREFACE

This book started innocently enough, with my writing the chapter "Going My Way." That was prompted by a vivid dream of reality, which brought back memories of a trip I took from Phu Bai to Da Nang in 1971. As I metaphorically rummaged through my duffel bag of memories, stories and images began to take focus as I continued to write. As all veterans do from time to time, I took a long and hard look at what might be in that metaphorical duffel bag, hence the name of this book. After writing two chapters, I sent them to Bob Toto, my longtime army buddy. Taking the bait, Bob joined in the writing effort.

To say this effort has been all-consuming would be correct. Bob and I recalled memories of past events and people long forgotten. As we dug deeper, we asked questions of one another, and suddenly we'd nail down the events as if they happened yesterday. As one may notice, we did not use real names for certain people. There are two reasons for this: The first would be to protect the guilty. The second would be that after about forty years, though I can see a face perfectly, I have sometimes forgotten the name.

Some people tend to embellish themselves when writing their memoirs. While we don't present ourselves as buffoons, we certainly don't show ourselves as all-knowing and ever-heroic. What we have presented here is an honest portrayal of two citizen soldiers trying to make it through the turbulent times of a country at war. This is also not just about Vietnam. In the ten-year period following the

Vietnam conflict, veterans who had seen and experienced the heavy combat from the fields of Southeast Asia wrote a plethora of books. Such books as *The Killing Zone*, by Frederick Downs, and *We Were Soldiers Once*, by Harold G. Moore and Joseph Galloway, are specific combat accounts describing the basic horrors of war in Vietnam. While the Vietnam experience, as Bob and I knew it, was dangerous and provided extended stress, it was by no means similar to the experiences described in the above books.

This compilation of stories represents history as seen from the mature eyes of veterans who were there on the ground of two battlefields. For those of you from the 1960s and 1970s who thought that there was only one war being fought, you are surely forgetful of what was happening during that time. It wasn't until much later that Bob and I realized that we were involved in two wars. As we thankfully trekked onto the soil of the Federal Republic of Germany, little did we know that we were entering a war zone at Frankfurt; albeit unlike Vietnam, it was a war zone nevertheless.

The war in Vietnam was primarily fought with weapons, hence the saying that we heard the "sounds of guns," which in army slang meant actual combat. Halfway around the world, another war was playing out its overture: the Cold War. The post-war world was playing out its legacy of the second half of the twentieth century. Because it is recent history, this set of stories represents a time and place in history that may be hard to understand only because it has not been analyzed in a true historical perspective.

The first write of history is done by the fourth estate, meaning the journalists on the ground observe current events. Later an analysis of events occurs. Upon further investigation, historians begin putting together the pieces of the puzzle and make the first historical analysis. Here is our historical perspective, which we have presented as honestly as we can. These actions and events essentially tell of a time that is past, never to be seen again. The draft is long gone, and along with it is a certain GI attitude and independent swagger of a certain cockiness that was indicative of the "citizen soldier."

The pre-volunteer army had big disadvantages and in general produced a less professional soldier with much less discipline. However, in many instances, we had highly intelligent soldiers who would never have served in a volunteer army. The following pages represent an appreciation of the times we experienced and how they have affected history, and in turn how we see things in the politics of the current times.

ORDER ARMS

This book required the efforts of two writers. It is a story encompassing the trials and tribulations of two officers of ROTC vintage who served their country during the Vietnam/Cold War era. As stated above, this soliloquy of explanation is our army command of "order arms." In army parlance "order arms" is a key rifle drill command placing the weapon at one's side. It is a sign of readiness and respect.

Since this book has two authors, there is a certain order as to the contents of this book. I primarily wrote the majority of the twenty-three chapters. However, in many of the chapters, Robert A. Toto brings in his perspective on events. These are labeled tongue-in-cheek as **Toto Moments**. Also in this effort, Bob has written his own chapters, which we have appropriately labeled the **Toto Chapters**. We wrote chronologically as we shared our experiences, both separately and together. One must remember that Bob and I were only together in the army protocol when we trained together in Fort Benning, Fort Bliss, and at the Jungle Warfare School in Panama. All other contacts were of a personal nature, whether in the United States, Germany, or Vietnam.

The timeline of these stories is from 1969 to 1972, and they depict the routines and stresses of what junior army officers faced as citizen soldiers. I hope you find this a revealing treatise that will spur further discussion.

Richard C. Geschke
Bristol, Connecticut
November 11, 2010

Sound Adjutant's Call

These memoirs have been written to both portray a very difficult time in history and to share stories from two army buddies. Pre-Vietnam influences were part of our culture: WWII, the A-bomb, Korea, the birth explosions, Joe McCarthy, the Cold War, the rise of the USSR, Sputnik, the race to space, the assassination of JFK, the march on Selma, the "peace" movement, riots on campuses, the music revolution, draft cards, burning bras, the death of RFK, and man landing on the moon.

We were young, as almost all soldiers are, fighting a war that no one wanted to fight. Such discord about Vietnam was almost as strong as the Civil War, where brother fought brother. Some people fled to Canada, others chose professions that were "exempted," and some didn't have a choice to make. Sure, our history influenced our behavior, but we were still young men trying to find our way in this turbulent and confusing time.

Hopefully, readers will assimilate our experiences, challenge our assumptions, and maybe pick up some new knowledge that will spur them to achievement. The 1960s were a revolutionary time, and the 1970s were a "magical mystery tour." I hope the reader will learn something from this tour as well.

Robert A. Toto
North Attleboro, Massachusetts
December 31, 2010

Acknowledgments

It was my son Scott who slowly persuaded me to write this book. As I have stated in the Preface, it started out with the chapter titled "Going My Way." As I delved into my duffel bag of memories, I found some things to be hazy and I was forced to call on my army buddy Bob Toto to refresh my memory. Before long I had Toto contributing anecdotes and chapters.

During these mad sessions of writing, my wife Ann was busy doing the first of many proofreads as my son was busy scanning forty-year-old pictures used in this book. Along the way I was starting to scatter my chapters to people who had the courage to read them. One of these people turned out to be Erma Odrach who was kind enough to read all of the manuscript and offer much-needed advice and encouragement.

More pictures were provided by Tom Couch and I called on the services of my good friend Dominika Sorensen who scanned and edited many of the pictures for publication. One picture in this book that didn't come from our personal collections was the one of the dreaded black palm. That great picture came to us from Timothy G. Davis with grateful thanks. The original basic idea for the cover was done by Jeremy Granger. Also to protect these writings my daughter Elizabeth Galletta Esq. a patent attorney, helped me navigate the hazardous trappings of copyright law. Other patient readers of this manuscript who offered encouragement and advice were William O'Brien, Paul Blood, Sean Lamb, and Gary Boudreau. Without the efforts of all the people mentioned above, I would never have rummaged through that duffel bag.

Chapter 1
Well, Toto, We Aren't
Civilians Anymore!

IOBC, it sounds like bullshit to me, to me.
IOBC, it sounds like bullshit to me.
They made me a second lieutenant,
They gave me two bars of gold,
They made me a forward observer,
And I lived to be two seconds old!

(Agility call sung to the tune of the refrain of "My Bonnie Lies over the Ocean")
Majority sentiment of the class of IOBC 10-70, Fort Benning, Georgia

We also had other songs or chants that we vocalized on the march, but none matched the intensity of "We Gotta Get out of This Place." We were young men being prepared to face the rigors and challenges of war. Make no mistake about it—all the training and indoctrination was trying to prepare us for our largest challenge. God help us all, here comes the citizen soldier.

Fort Benning, Georgia
November 1969

Y ou know, I did have a choice when it came to serving my country. I could have gone the route of teaching, thus gaining a deferment. I never truly figured why I went the route I

1

did. It definitely wasn't for the money. In reality, it was probably curiosity and a desire to learn the ropes of leadership that led me on the long and difficult path of the next twenty-eight months. What I experienced during this time span provided an education that was much more extensive and complete than my previous four years of matriculating at Kent State University. I graduated in August of 1969, and upon receiving my degree, I was awarded two bars of gold, becoming a second lieutenant in the US Army Reserve. With this, I received orders to report to Fort Benning on November 1, 1969, for the Infantry Officer Basic Course (IOBC).

Heading for Adventure

I was a young kid who had never flown in an airplane before, and here I was, in uniform, on a plane to my ultimate destination of Fort Benning, Georgia. At that point, my military career was nothing but a blank sheet of paper. The entries on that paper over the next twenty-eight months would provide adventure, boredom, phonies, insight, mistakes, and above all, unforgettable memories.

While I do remember the plane trip, I only faintly remember the bus trip to Columbus, Georgia, which was the city outside Fort Benning. My first impression of this huge military installation was favorable. The buildings and officers' barracks reminded me of a college campus. Reporting for duty, I was assigned a room to share with a National Guard second lieutenant by the name of Weaver. I immediately organized my belongings, and once finished, I wandered off to the second-floor portico, which offered an excellent view of the entire complex containing the officers' barracks. It was early evening, and dusk was creeping into the complex, but the area was well lit so one could see all the comings and goings. Off in the distant twilight appeared to be a young second lieutenant struggling with his baggage, trying to locate his assigned quarters. As I saw a young Lieutenant Robert Toto trying to negotiate the portico, I, in my sympathy for this worn-out young man, helped him carry his things to his assigned room. Forty-two years later, Bob and I are still close friends. Many of my other army acquaintances are long forgotten, but Toto and I became lifetime army buddies.

Lieutenant Geschke
Fort Benning, November 1969

Welcome to Infantry Officer Basic (IOBC)

The cadre welcomed us to the wonderments of IOBC 10-70. This would last ten weeks in an attempt to inspire, educate, and create what Fort Benning is known to do, and that is produce a class of well-trained professional infantry officers. As the class acclimated to the routine, we became acutely aware that our training was pointed to future operations in the Republic of Vietnam. Our classes covered everything from military courtesy to calling in artillery fire in actual live field conditions.

All instructors were Vietnam veterans, and to be honest, most were very good. Since I didn't want to become one of those junior officer casualties, I did maintain a high level of attention. As is always the case in the military, the training after any length of time becomes mind-numbing and highly repetitive. In fact, whether it was on the use of M1A1 toilet paper or land navigation, each class seemed to start with the familiar refrain of "If you don't pay attention to the uses of _____, you will probably die in Vietnam." In the old army, you had to watch out for M-1 thumb when bolting a weapon's chamber. In IOBC in 1969, you had to watch out for the dreaded "If you don't learn this, you will die in Vietnam." Such was the cross that all young lieutenants had to bear at Fort Benning. This old, familiar refrain became imbedded into the culture of Fort Benning, Georgia, circa 1969.

Don't Go Out and Buy Any Long-Playing Records!

It wasn't until the ninth week of our training that we had two instructors who knew how to get our attention. This block of instruction was called "Calling in artillery fire." As I remember, the instructors were captains wearing their CIBs (Combat Infantryman Badges) with ranger tabs and airborne wings (paratroopers), which were the normal accoutrements for instructors at the Benning School for boys. These two didn't threaten us with the usual refrain of "You will die in Vietnam." Their spiel honestly caught our attention, and it went something like this:

> *Gentlemen, we know that in every one of your classes, you have been told that if you don't pay attention and learn about the key points of the class that you will die in Vietnam. No, no, we refuse to tell you this. However, what we will tell you is that if you don't learn the basic rudiments of calling in effective artillery fire, we wouldn't recommend that you go out and buy any long-playing records!*

En route to the training, live artillery rounds were fired over our heads. They sounded like freight trains pulsating wind over our heads. Our instructors told us that if we heard a round, we were okay … The one that was earmarked for us was the soundless, deadly killer. You can bet the house that every lieutenant took an active interest in performing to the best of his abilities the basic tenets of calling in effective artillery fire.

Bozos and Military Lifers (Hopeless Lifelong Soldiers)

As time went by, the usual military rhythm took effect. Within the rigorous routine, some of my peers knew what they were doing, and then there were the others. As for myself, I had serious doubts regarding my qualifications, but I started to gain confidence that I could do the job. We had young men with drinking problems ... and others who physically couldn't operate under field conditions. We had a lieutenant who couldn't throw a grenade over the concrete barrier protecting him. During a night firing exercise, one other lieutenant couldn't change an M-14 magazine (yes, we trained with M-14s, when we would be using M-16s in Vietnam—ah, the army in all its infinite wisdom) during rapid fire. We had all sizes and shapes from all over the country, and I could honestly say that half of them I would follow as leaders, and the other half did not show any leadership qualities. By the end of training, I knew that Toto and I belonged—not that we were professionals, but rather simply put, we were competent managers.

As the training progressed, we spent most of our free time hanging around officers' clubs, where we met with other students who were at Fort Benning for airborne, ranger, and pathfinder training. That was where combat veterans embellished their combat stories. One such incident occurred at a small O-Club (officers club) annex on a Saturday night. A rather senior captain, fortified by drink, called for a toast from all the junior officers in attendance, stating, "To those battling troopers of Dien Bien Phu who died with their boots on!" As I rolled my eyes at Toto, I honestly wondered what had made me go down this path of military madness. Were all of them that crazy?

This Southern Turkey Gets Revenge!

When we had a weekend off for Thanksgiving, Toto, Weaver, and I took a bus trip to Atlanta to get off base. Atlanta wasn't the international city that it is today, but it had restaurants and topless bars. We ate our Thanksgiving meal at a local restaurant. Toto and I had turkey—what else? Weaver had duck. Toto and I got food poisoning; we should never have left Fort Benning.

5

There's an Old Army Saying: "Never Volunteer."

At the time of the Vietnam conflict in late 1969, the country was severely split as to our participation, and the pressure was on Nixon to withdraw the troops. Coincidently, during this time span, Lieutenant William Calley's story of the My Lai Massacre was just breaking, and Calley resided at Fort Benning. Toto and I saw Calley migrating with his entourage to the dining hall at the Fort Benning O-Club several days a week. His companions were a myriad of JAG (Judge Advocate General) Corps lawyers preparing for his subsequent trial, which would take place a year later, in November of 1970. What was particularly curious was a rather large individual who followed at a distance. He was not military, and we assumed that he was Lieutenant Calley's bodyguard.

While all this was transpiring, Bob and I weren't relishing the fact that in a few short weeks, we were going to our first stateside duty station to serve for four to six months before transferring to South Vietnam for a one-year tour of duty. This was the common protocol for infantry officers at that time in history. The army had a bait-and-switch scam that enticed Bob and me to sign under the auspices of "voluntary indefinite" to assure a guaranteed one-year assignment to anywhere where there were infantry units of the US Army. It was our hope that during this one-year span, Nixon would withdraw combat forces and our tours would be completed in the noncombat zone of the friendly confines of West Germany. The term "vol indef" would live throughout our military careers, and it was a time bomb that would explode eighteen months later.

Toto and I signed our lives away much as in the story of *The Devil and Daniel Webster*. We had hopes of serving the rest of our military careers in some remote German outpost, which was wishful thinking at best. In the interim of shipping out to Germany, Toto and I spent a month in Fort Bliss at the Redeye Missile School.

Bob and I finally finished our training at Fort Benning. Not only did we bid adieu to Fort Benning, but we were also exiting the turbulent 1960s. For that moment, we only saw the southern road before us as we traveled with our classmate Lieutenant Thomas Couch on our way to Fort Bliss. As we, the Three Stooges, left, little did we know that all three of us would reunite to continue our illustrious military careers in the Federal Republic of Germany.

Lieutenants Weaver (left) and Toto (right)
Fort Benning, January 1970

CHAPTER 2
THE WINDS OF CHANGE

A s we exited Fort Benning, we were saying good-bye to the sixties, but we were also about to enter the realm of paying the piper for the mistakes of wise men who were considered by many to be the best and brightest. We would be taken in a new and vigorous direction. By the end of the decade, America found itself in a savage war in Southeast Asia. These wise men no longer had all the answers, and people were growing restless. So when Bob and I were leaving Fort Benning a decade later, we were mere fodder thrown into the abyss to continue the folly of mistakes in Southeast Asia. The only right thing these leaders of the sixties did was continue the Cold War policies of détente and defensive posturing. It was in Southeast Asia that these leaders took the wrong fork in the road.

The New Frontier

To me, the 1960s were ushered in a little after noon on an extremely sunny afternoon on January 20, 1961, by John F. Kennedy. The following words created the mood and feeling of a new and energized nation, which Kennedy would later refer to as the "New Frontier":

> *We dare not forget today that we are the heirs of that first revolution. Let the word go forth from this time and place, to friend and foe alike, that the torch has been passed to a new generation of Americans—born in this century, tempered by*

war, disciplined by a hard and bitter peace, proud of our ancient heritage, and unwilling to witness or permit the slow undoing of those human rights to which this nation has always been committed, and to which we are committed today at home and around the world.

The decade would start with *Leave It to Beaver* and *Ozzie and Harriet*, and it would end with *The Mod Squad* and Neil Armstrong walking on the moon. What transpired in between changed America faster in the sphere of politics and social decorum than in any previous decade. Change is the essence of history. The studies of political, social, and cultural changes represent historical perspectives of things as they evolve. When we look at a periodical, we can ascertain by fashion, advertisements, use of language, and the modes of transportation in what time period it was printed. As technology rapidly increased, change occurred at a faster pace. Radios were in vogue until TVs came into play. Cars transformed from the dowdy to having swept-wing fins. Things began to change at a much faster pace. President Kennedy promised that we would land on the moon within ten years, and he was right. In essence, the 1960s seemed to explode in all areas, not only in the technological realm but also in the political, social, and cultural disciplines.

Rapid Changes

Is all change good? Ask a Jew if the changes of the German government in the 1930s were good. Ask a Chinese person if the Cultural Revolution served his purposes. Ask an infantryman at the battle of Hue in 1968 if change helped his outlook on life. As you see, change can be good, it can be bad, and it can be neither good nor bad. With this in mind, it's time to analyze the above words of JFK's speech and see if what he said and foresaw in the changing scene of America was indeed factual, if the future of what he visualized came to be. Remember, at the time, these words were inspiring and patriotic, showing a proud heritage with the hope for a prouder future.

The first section of our study begins with the following: "We dare not forget that we are the heirs of that first revolution." JFK was correct; our government, with its adherence to democracy, has been passed to us, and we are the heirs to that continuance of democracy.

The Greatest Generation?

"Let the word go forth from this time and place, to friend and foe alike, that the torch has been passed to a new generation of Americans ..." JFK was telling us that a new and younger generation is now in power—and letting the world know that the guard has changed from the old to the young.

In the next portion of this paragraph, JFK explains the facts of his new administration: "Born in this century, tempered by war, disciplined by a hard and bitter peace, proud of our ancient heritage ..."

This is what Tom Brokaw would call the "Greatest Generation" thirty-seven years later. It was Brokaw's thesis that of all generations in the realm of American history, this generation was the greatest, bravest, and most influential of all. As outlined in his book, Brokaw's theory tells of a people that lived through the Great Depression and went on to fight as citizen soldiers in the epic struggle that was World War II, claiming that their sacrifices and accomplishments exceed all other American generations by far.

JFK was indeed espousing this generation in his address. This generation was also vigilant in its duty to maintain the peace in the postwar world of détente. What President Kennedy was indicating was that the old guard of such august men as Eisenhower, Truman, Churchill, and so forth, was passing from the political scene, and a new and vigorous dynamic generation born in the twentieth century was here to forge ahead and lead the free world down the yellow brick road.

In the ever-changing dynamic that was the sixties, we see the greatest generation's leadership skills and decisions put to the severe test in politics, social changes, and the dynamics of a fast-changing world that had spun out of control. With all the good and the sacrifices made by JFK's generation, their governance of the

American dynamic in their mature productive years would fall short of the moniker that Mr. Brokaw so proudly promoted. Our leaders born in the prior century were more tempered, flexible, and willing to change direction in crisis. Roosevelt (both of them), Marshall, Truman, and (in Great Britain) Sir Winston Churchill were effective leaders who led by example and were willing to change direction when the climate called for change.

Let's Not Flatter Ourselves!

For me, the last part of our study of JFK's speech holds the most controversy of what America truly was in 1961. The words are stirring, patriotic, and would make all Americans proud. However, upon closer scrutiny, do these words really hold up in retrospect? In assessing the following closure of this paragraph, I found it to contain both truths and untruths: "And unwilling to witness or permit the slow undoing of those human rights to which the nation has always been committed, and to which we are committed today at home and around the world."

These are indeed lofty ideals and inspirational words. At that time in history, America was committed to the betterment of lives in Europe with the Marshall Plan, the Truman Doctrine, the Berlin Airlift, and the institution of NATO. Uncle Sam, as seen through the eyes of a person in postwar Europe, saw a benevolent super power helping it rebuild from the world's worst disaster. However, Kennedy's reference to our always advocating human rights at home doesn't hold water. His words were essentially nothing more than political propaganda that doesn't contain the whole truth, so help you God. In John Toland's masterful book *Adolph Hitler*, the following was written:

> *Hitler's concept of concentration camps as well as the practicality owed much, so he claimed, to his studies of English and United States history. He admired the camps for Boer prisoners in South Africa and for the Indians in the Wild West; and often praised to his inner circle the efficiency of America's extermination by starvation and uneven combat of the red savages who could not be tamed by captivity.*

11

So much for human rights throughout our history.

As JFK spoke these words, the KKK was still active, and the riots protesting civil liberties in major US cities, including Washington, were still far in the future. As inspiring as these words were, not all of them are true, nor were they historically accurate. Inspirational rhetoric based on hopes and political contrivance can sound good, but looking closer, it may be no more than political advertising.

On the other end of the spectrum, we can analyze the speeches of Winston Churchill and Abraham Lincoln, both master wordsmiths of the English language, and find nothing but accurate and meaningful substance meant for cognitive thinking of current events. It must be noted that neither Churchill nor Lincoln had speechwriters; they authored their own speeches. President Kennedy, on the other hand, relied on speechwriters, most notably Theodore White and his Harvard cadre of advisers, to craft his thoughts. Kennedy's delivery was impeccable, whereas Churchill and Lincoln delivered their thoughts not as political commercials but as sincere efforts to inform their constituents.

True Wordsmiths

First, let's look at the famous speech Churchill made to the king on May 13, 1940, in the House of Commons, upon his acceptance as prime minister of Great Britain. His speech reflected his thoughts concerning Great Britain, and all he told his constituents was that it wouldn't be easy. The enemy was bad, and he had no good news to offer, saying that they must bear the burden together. The following is the highlight of this great oratory:

> *I would say to the House, as I said to those who have joined this Government: I have nothing to offer but blood, toil, tears, and sweat.*

> *We have before us an ordeal of the most grievous kind. We have before us many, many months of struggle and suffering. You ask, what is our policy? I can say: It is to wage war, by sea, land and air, with all our might and with all the strength God can give us; to wage war against a monstrous tyranny, never surpassed*

in the dark, lamentable catalogue of human crime. That is our policy.

Churchill's speech didn't pull any punches and wasn't meant to win friends and influence people. It stated the bare facts: here we are, things are not that great, we intend to fight, and our enemy is the devil himself. This rhetoric was all fact, no fiction, and Churchill himself wrote it.

On to President Lincoln, who in 1865, at his inaugural, had to convince the American people to let bygones be bygones. In the following select sentences, we see that Lincoln wanted to mend all fences with everyone. One year later, the Fourteenth Amendment would be written, and the road to the abolishment of slavery and the use of a democratic government would indeed take place. Lincoln would not live long enough to witness the first baby steps of the acceptance of the Negro race in assimilation to the American way of life. The following words would go a long way to persuade the Southern leadership to acquiesce and treat the Negro problem. Lincoln would not live to see the results of his hopes in this speech. But unlike Kennedy, his goals were factual and true, with no made-up rhetoric. The following is what Lincoln said:

> *With malice toward none; with charity for all; with firmness in the right, as God gives us to see the right, let us strive on to finish the work we are in; to bind up the nation's wounds; to care for him who shall have borne the battle, and for his widow, and his orphan—to do all which may achieve and cherish a just and lasting peace, among ourselves, and with all nations.*

The political and business leaders of this Greatest Generation were to keep some of the policies and practices of the old guard. Regarding the Cold War in Europe, the long, hard winter would continue on its road with destiny and ultimate victory. It was in other areas both socially and politically where JFK's generation failed. Their adherence to the falling domino theory and their quantitative approach to Southeast Asia proved to be the fatal bullet. The so-called best and brightest cadre formed under Kennedy and utilized by Lyndon Johnson adhered to unproven theories and were aided by sycophants who turn out to be mere yes-men.

Richard C. Geschke and Robert A. Toto

The Insightful Fourth Estate

David Halberstam brought forth these perspectives as he wrote about what transpired while he was a reporter in Vietnam. A whole generation of journalists whom I call tweeners began reporting for all to read and hear about what was happening all around us. Halberstam, Woodward, and Bernstein were a new breed of writers who showed what happened and refused to be persuaded by the status quo of the Greatest Generation. Halberstam was on the ground and reported the happenings in South Vietnam factually. He found out that our American leadership was not reporting the actual happenings. General Harkins was playing a confidence game that would continue under the auspices of General Westmoreland. Halberstam saw this and reported truthfully what transpired.

Woodward and Bernstein were like pit bulls who stuck to tracking the truth of Watergate; they did not compromise. And kudos to Katherine Graham for running these true and factual reports of the reporters. I call them tweeners because by their birthdates, they would not see active combat in the conscript armed services. They were too young for Korea and too old for Vietnam.

A Frightful Schism in Time

Through the sixties, great changes took place: JFK was assassinated; there was the Gulf of Tonkin Resolution and the escalation of the Vietnam conflict; Martin Luther King led a movement of civil rights and was assassinated; there were race riots, the TET Offensive, the My Lai Massacre, and ugly campus protests; and the United States won the race to the moon. During these happenings, I attended high school, graduated from Kent State University in 1969, joined ROTC, received my degree and my commission in the US Army Reserve, and worked in the steel mills of the flats of Cleveland, awaiting my turn, as past generations had, to become a citizen soldier. Little did I know that I would be the last generation to be in a non-volunteer army and serving in a major armed conflict. It wasn't like being in my father's army of twenty-seven years before my entry into the army. While many people approved of my uniform, just as many people detested the sight of it.

14

CHAPTER 3
TRAVELING FIRST CLASS—ARMY STYLE

W hen I look back at January and February of 1970, all I see are wide stretches of open road, a Mexico border town, a smidgen of military instruction, more open road, and the unforgettable Thomas (T.) Couch. His hometown of Houston, Texas, was our next destination. Tom Couch graduated with Bob and me from Infantry Officer Basic School. Our plan was to tag along with Tom to Houston in his brand-new car. We would then proceed to take a bus from Houston to El Paso, where our next school was located at Fort Bliss.

Following the Gulf Coast

Our trek started at the gates of Fort Benning. We traveled through Georgia, Alabama, Mississippi, Louisiana, and on to Houston, Texas. Our epic journey shadowed the Gulf Coast all day and into the night and the next morning. The travel arrangements were choreographed by the eminent T. Couch, whose habits included smoking cigarettes as we did, but he had the unusual habit of snuffing out the butt on the floor mat of his new car. Among other Couchisms were spinning Texas tall tales in the charming Southern drawl that emanated from his six-foot-four-inch frame. His mannerisms were all rather teddy bearish and not in any way to be confused with the usual demeanor of a second lieutenant in the infantry. Tom was heading home prior to reporting to Fort Benjamin Harrison for PIO (Public Information

Office) class before he too would proceed to Germany. Toto and I were headed to Redeye Missile School and widening our spectrum of combat weapons systems, whereas Couch was honing his journalistic talents. Now who was the smart one in choosing our military options? Was it the charming good old boy with the made-up drawl or the two city slickers? Way down the road, you will see the results of this leading question.

Giving the Finger!

As we continued down the road, we decided to share the driving. Just as we arrived in Louisiana, Couch stopped to make the switch of drivers, passing the baton to me. No problem: we'd stop, switch drivers, and move on. However, with Couch, nothing was simple. The adventure began as he caught his hand in the glide system that adjusted the seating. Have you ever heard a coyote yelp? All six feet four inches of T. Couch let out a scream, which I do believe is still hovering above the bayous of Louisiana to this day, as his finger was wedged between the glider and the seat. He was in obvious pain, and Toto and I had to literally shoulder into the seat from the rear to un-jam his finger. With this accomplished, we sought medical assistance for Texas T. We ended up at highway patrol headquarters to assist our wounded comrade. Now that I think of it, Couch should have been awarded the Purple Finger for his heroics, although I don't believe that is an officially authorized medal. I can picture the injured finger in the known *finger pose* in a purple haze; that would be appropriate for Couch.

Moving Trees and Cajun Gumbo

The trek continued down the coast road, and Toto commented that as he was driving later that evening that the trees were moving out into the road. Just to let you know, none of us took drugs; we were getting tired and hungry. It was time for a break, and Couch had the perfect remedy for our driving blues. We were running parallel to bayou country, and as old T. Couch put it, we were in desperate need of some good old-fashioned Cajun gumbo. Quite soon enough, off to our immediate right was an old run-down Southern-style diner. As The Three Stooges entered the diner, we looked like fish out of water; old T. Couch began to exaggerate his Southern drawl, which was actually changing to a Cajun twang. As we headed to our seats, Couch immediately began to charm the middle-aged waitress into getting three bowls of genuine Cajun gumbo. As I recollect, it was damn good!

Well fed, we continued our trip with the trees jumping out at us all along this southern route. Nevertheless, we arrived at the Couch residence sometime the next morning. After we were fed and had slept the sleep of the dead, we trekked down the road, via Greyhound, toward the destination of the San Antonio home of Fort Sam Houston. You may be asking what was at Fort Sam Houston. My high school buddy Gary Tomcho was stationed there with his wife. Gary was a medic who had served a tour at Chu Lai, Vietnam, in a medivac unit. As Toto and I visited Gary, we had to endure more war stories and advice for us junior officers destined for Southeast Asia. We bid adieu to Fort Sam and headed to the remote outpost on the southern tip of Texas, Fort Bliss.

No Room at the Inn

As we wearily stepped off the bus and sauntered into the post of Fort Bliss, we were told directly that there was no room at the inn for junior lieutenants seeking quarters for the Redeye Missile School. As Toto and I were beginning to realize, the army, in all its infinite wisdom, was beginning to be our major roadblock. We had to look for off-post housing, which we did. We found a place, but this presented a new problem: how were we to get to the post every day? To Toto's amazement, we found ourselves at a VW dealership, where I bought a brand-new powder-blue VW Bug. This not only answered our immediate transportation problems but would be used as our vehicle on our continued trek. In fact, that car was destined to be taken back to Germany to drive on the autobahn in its home country. Talk about taking coals to Newcastle!

Army Life on the Soft Side!

The course was a four-week primer into all the facets of this first-generation heat-seeking shoulder-held guided missile system. In all honesty, the four weeks turned into an easy vacation for all concerned. Gone were the harassing and menacing instructors. These courses were conducted by ADA (Air Defense Artillery) instructors who took a low-key and almost gentle approach to military decorum.

Our basic day stretched from 09:00 to 17:00, five days a week. As far as Bob and I were concerned, this was the army as it should be. We learned all facets of the Redeye Missile. We learned how to fire the weapon, maintain the weapon, store the weapon; we learned how to tactically employ the weapon, and how to train people in the uses of the weapon. It was a virtual smorgasbord of the Redeye Missile unplugged. Much to the chagrin of every air force pilot within thirty miles, we were drilled in aircraft recognition (so we wouldn't shoot the missile at our own guys). We had to pass with a 90 percent on the air recognition test. I guess a 10-percent loss was considered collateral damage. Enough about our love affair with the Redeye Missile. Now on to the good part.

South of the Border

There was a potpourri of fun stuff to do. We frequented the racetrack in Juarez, Mexico, with its cheap drinks and dog races. We became regulars, and as I remember it, we won more than we lost. We took in other Mexican attractions, including an amateur bullfight in which Toto and I upset the locals when we were caught rooting for the bull. And in rather classic border-town episodes, we haggled with the merchants for their merchandise. Also, as I recall, other "merchandise" was peddled: youngsters hawked the wares of "young ladies" to the gringos by claiming that their mothers were indeed virgins. Those four weeks went by fast, and soon it was time to pack the Bug and head north. Bob and I decided to visit my home in Cleveland and his home in Methuen, Massachusetts, before heading out for our first permanent tours in Germany.

Heading to the Great Lakes

It is now decades later, and as I'm retracing our trip from Fort Bliss to my parents' house on the west side of Cleveland, Ohio, I'm simply amazed. I consulted MapQuest, and while the route recommend was different from our 1970 routing, I was flabbergasted that it showed it to be 1,793 miles away, with an estimated travel time of twenty-seven hours and five minutes. Bob and I drove nonstop, going about 1,900 miles in a little over thirty-three hours. It's a good thing we were young and didn't know any better, because in retracing this episode, I truly don't know how we did this.

Since we got a late start out of Fort Bliss, which was at about 10:30 hours, all our best plans to stay overnight in St. Louis later turned to naught. The Bug was filled to the gills, and we had to put our suitcases on the luggage rack on top of the car. As we headed north through the arid lands of the Texas desert, the car struggled up slight inclines in which we were doing sixty miles per hour at most. When we hit the flatlands, we cruised at seventy or seventy-five miles per hour. Even at seventy-five miles per hour we were nowhere near the speed limit as during this time period there was no speed limit in the desert flatlands of Texas. During our long, monotonous journey, we kept getting into wind gusts that would literally push the car in whatever direction. One such gust nearly had us hydroplaning in a slight rainstorm, and the suitcases on the luggage rack blew off the car and exploded onto the desert highway. Toto and I scrambled to secure our lost suitcases. Not only did we have to worry about being pushed around by windstorms, but we also had to watch that the Texas desert didn't take all our belongings as we traveled through it. There was some excitement as we muddled on through Texas in search of the Buckeye State, which was still a long way in the distance.

To hell with staying the night in St. Louis. We didn't arrive there until 08:00 hours. We didn't need to sleep, did we? We hit southern Ohio, around the Dayton area, at about 14:00 hours and knew it was time to switch drivers, as Bob was due for some shuteye. I took over, though tired and exhausted, and as I started my leg of the trip, I figured it would end triumphantly, with my driving into Cleveland as the long-lost hero. It didn't take long, much to Toto's chagrin, before

I started to tear up and had to pull over to the side of I-71. Tears were running down my face, and Bob got the message that I couldn't continue driving. He had to do a double shift. As we got further north, though, I did take over, driving to the residence of Carl F. Geschke, situated in the West Park section of Cleveland, Ohio. When we got into the house, my father, with a cigar in his mouth, looked at us as we sat down. "You both look like shit!" he declared. He had a bottle in his hand and offered Bob and me a drink. Within thirty minutes, both of us were dead to the world.

I drove up the driveway of my parents' house as a twenty-three-year-old kid. My parents had been married twenty-nine years. My father was a steelworker and would retire within the next eighteen months after thirty long years on the job. My mother, Ethel A. Geschke, who had spent most of her life as a domestic engineer, was working at a local Marriot motel at the time. Both of my parents were born and raised in Cleveland, Ohio, as second-generation transplants from Europe. They raised two sons in the middle-class section of West Park. Even as a World War II veteran of three and a half years, my father had never left the States. His army unit, a tank destroyer battalion, was so good in field exercises that they were used to train other units. My parents were hardworking, God-fearing, and industrious, putting the education of their sons above everything else. I was the first of our side of the family to graduate from college.

At this time, Cleveland was in an economic downturn that would last another twenty years. Cleveland was an industrial city, dependent on the steel and automotive industries. The years of polluting the adjacent rivers and Lake Erie were beginning to take an environmental toll. In a few short years, people would be losing jobs, businesses would literally go south, and the very operating government of the City of Cleveland would be bankrupt. It wouldn't be until the mid-1990s that Cleveland would transform itself into a new and dynamic entity.

Such was the prevailing way of life as we spent a few days in the lands of the Western Reserve. Essentially, I took Bob to meet my friends and old haunts. We perused the old burlesque house of The Roxy, and Toto was stunned that the girls actually took it all off. In retrospect, as I thought about where we went and what we did, it was as if we were looking at the last vestiges of the old postwar world, which was indeed evaporating into a new era. The old haunts created by old industrial prosperity were becoming long in the tooth. The baby boom generation was up and coming, and their attitudes were different and often rebellious. Woodstock had already transpired, the Kent State shootings were in the future, and Nixon was being forced to consider withdrawing troops from Vietnam. Bob and I were glad to be wearing civilian clothes, and in most instances, we didn't volunteer the fact that we were in the military.

Heading Toward New England

At the time, I knew this would be my last visit home in a long while—this in fact was my good-bye to my old way of life. Toto got the meaning of my background and culture. Looking into the future, our next stop was Toto's home in Methuen, Massachusetts. We were on the road again. So long Cleveland; onward to the great state of the Commonwealth of Massachusetts.

We drove onto I-90, pointed due northeast toward northern New York. On the plains of the Finger Lakes south of Rochester and Syracuse, we drove into several whiteout snowstorms. This time we weren't dodging moving trees; we were trying to avoid the snowflakes all the way to New England. As usual, Bob and I shared the driving, and at the present day, MapQuest states that we traveled approximately 656 miles. I'll take their word for it.

Bob's parents had just moved into a development of new homes in Methuen. As we drove into the driveway of the bi-level home, I was greeted by the same middle-class family that had waved good-bye to me in Ohio. Bob's father was a WWII veteran of the Italian Campaign with the Thirty-Fourth Infantry Division and had seen combat. Fred Toto was made of the same stuff as my father. Both were products of the Depression era and had acquired wisdom with their street smarts. Bob's mother, Pauline, was built of the same stuff as my own mother. Now, over four decades later, all of our parents have passed. In June of 2010, my mother, at the age of ninety-two, was the last to leave us. The last of the Mohicans!

Bob schlepped me around to visit his friends and relatives, just as I had done with him back in Cleveland. Bob was saying the same good-byes I was. Family affairs consumed our time, and as quick as a wink, we were planning to take my car to Bayonne, New Jersey, to be shipped to Bremerhaven in West Germany. Coals to Newcastle!

Completing the Circle

According to MapQuest, it's 247 miles from Methuen to Bayonne. No sweat, right? Have you ever traveled through New York City? In 1970, the megalopolis was there in all its Eastern Seaboard reality. It took us forever, but we finally hit a local flophouse outside Bayonne, New Jersey, where we spent the night. The next morning, we were in Bayonne, with my orders to ship the powder-blue Bug to Bremerhaven. Shortly thereafter, we headed to the Newark airport, where we boarded a plane headed to Charleston, South Carolina. Toto and I climbed aboard to our final US destination. Once we arrived at Charleston, things happened fast. Toto got his flight quickly to Germany. I stayed behind, but the next morning I too was headed to Frankfurt. The real army awaited both of us as we landed in Germany. By the way, the long and winding road was a little over 5,000 miles, 4,300 of them spent driving a car!

CHAPTER 4
WEST GERMANY: IN THE SHADOWS
OF THE IRON CURTAIN

*From Stettin in the Baltic to Trieste in the Adriatic, an iron
curtain has descended across the Continent.*
—*Winston S. Churchill*
"The Sinews of Peace" March 5, 1946
Westminster College, Fulton, Missouri

A s the plane lifted off from Charleston, heading northeast
to Frankfurt, Germany, my thoughts were not initially on
my next duty station. Instead, I was thinking of the joy of
knowing I was going in the opposite direction of the sounds of guns.
However, as the plane approached Germany, my thoughts turned to
just where I was going ... and whether this trip was truly necessary.
The plane landed at Frankfurt in early March of 1970, which was
almost twenty-five years since the guns had been silenced for the
last time in twentieth-century Germany. The Federal Republic of
Germany was in existence for twenty-one years as a direct result of
the Potsdam Agreement of 1945. In fact, with the formation of West
Germany, along with this new government entity, began the realities
of the Cold War.

A Divided Germany

After World War II, Germany was divided into four zones, which

23

were controlled by the United States, Great Britain, France, and the USSR. To complicate this further, Berlin, which was located in the Russian zone, was also divided by the same four powers. While technically the division of the four zones of Germany ended with the formation of the Federal Republic of Germany (West Germany) and the German Democratic Republic (East Germany) in 1949, all the powers remained in place except France, and the Cold War began with a rather innocent sneeze. However, with that sneeze came the runny nose, along with the usual aches and pains. Stalin began solidifying Russian influence over all of Eastern Europe, keeping an ironclad grip on the pulse of the Eastern governments, especially East Germany.

The Cold War moved on, with Russian control in the east, and there were two major revolts in the 1950s: the first in East Berlin in 1953, and the second in Hungary in 1956. Later, in the 1960s, the Berlin Wall and the construction of a fenced barrier along its western borders, resulting in the completion of Churchill's metaphorical Iron Curtain, clearly set the manifestation of what the Cold War was all about. Communism had set up barriers not only of the mind but also as very real walls to prevent its citizens from leaving.

As real as the physical barriers of walls and fences were, the differences of political ideology are what proved to be the true essence of the Cold War. In 1968, a major revolt in Czechoslovakia was brutally put down by the Soviet Union. In this conflict, which manifested itself in psychological and economic warfare, political and propaganda rhetoric were exchanged; it seemed that this contest would continue into perpetuity. The KGB and CIA intelligence organizations were creating their own fiefdoms as the true soldiers of the Cold War. A whole genre of movies was created around the Cold War antics, much to the delight of fiction writers, movie producers, and screen actors.

Political Divisions

The city of Berlin turned into a mysterious and much-desired city to watch and monitor during the years of the Cold War. So when I arrived in Frankfurt, Germany, on that March day in 1970,

I was two generations removed from the end of Nazi Germany. The infrastructure of West Germany was completely rebuilt. West Germany governed themselves, without outside influence, and they became an integral part of the European and world economy. The people were trying to distance themselves from their shame of Nazi Germany. Their pride was beginning to show itself again; their political gait was returning.

As I would soon find out when I arrived at my duty station in Aschaffenburg, the culture and attitudes of the US military presence continued in the post–World War II mind-set. GIs were issued ration books for gasoline, coffee, butter, hard liquor, and cigarettes. The merchandise sold in the PX (post exchange) was much sought after by the local populace. In fact, a small black market economy was deeply imbedded into the West German economy. Prices of certain items, such as gasoline and cigarettes, were much higher than what an American GI would pay for them at the local PX. The metric system was used to blend in instead of the American measurement system. You were issued gasoline vouchers in liters, based on the horsepower of the vehicle you used. The price was one-fourth of what the locals paid. Hence there was rationing so as not to adversely affect the West German economy. It should be noted that the entire western zone of Germany was inundated with the American and British military presence.

Zoning In

The bases occupied by both the British and American units were called "kasernes." These were usually old Wehrmacht installations taken over by the Allies after World War II. The American presence was concentrated in Bavaria, which was located in the southwest German zone. The British zone of influence was in the northwest German zone. Across the fenced barrier of the Iron Curtain, running due east of West Germany, Mother Russia and the East German Army were guarding the borders. On one side, the sunshine of freedom showed a prosperous and thriving political entity recovering from an almost fatal blow. On the other side, we saw the darkness of a political entity that perpetuated a way of life that in the future would evaporate from existence because it's very essence of being was based on a lie.

A Toto Moment

Stationed in West Berlin, we were many miles from the East German border. As Dick mentioned, the United States did not recognize East Germany as a sovereign country. Therefore, our trips into West Germany were referred to as "going to the zone." Leaving West Berlin was via the autobahn by car, from Templehof Airport by air (via one of the three air corridors agreed to by the Potsdam Agreement), or by the "duty train." More about that later.

I was told to wait at the repo depot (replacement unit), as it was called, and an officer would pick me up from my future army unit. Within the hour, I was met by a first lieutenant who was driving an American car. As we loaded my duffel bag into his car, he began describing the infantry battalion I was assigned to and the town of Aschaffenburg, where the unit was located. Soon enough, I learned I was to become a "cotton baler" in the First Battalion, Seventh Infantry in the Third Brigade of the Third Infantry Division. The First of the Seventh was located in Aschaffenburg, in the old Wermacht quarters of Graves Kaserne. The GIs referred to Aschaffenburg as A'Burg, which was home to five major kasernes, thus becoming a town of significant American military presence. In 1970, the population of A'Burg was approximately fifty-five thousand people, and it was situated in the picturesque setting of Northern Bavaria.

A Toto Moment

My trip to West Berlin began from the replacement company in Frankfurt. Once I convinced the sergeant first class in charge that my orders did not specify a unit, I learned that I was going to West Berlin, and I pleaded gross ignorance as to my knowledge of the geography of Germany. I knew I was quite a distance from Berlin, and I asked how I was to travel to Berlin. The sergeant informed me, "You will go there via the duty train." Well, the only visions of an American troop train I had were from Hollywood. I had images of soldiers hanging out of windows, while loose women constricted themselves around drunken GIs. This was definitely not the case.

A bus took me to the main Frankfurt train terminal (bahnhof) just as rush hour began. Everyone was speaking German, except me, and I looked around for any signs of the army or the red, white, and blue of Uncle Sam. Suddenly, while dragging my duffel bag containing all my worldly possessions behind me, I saw an American flag. I lowered my head, thanked God, and headed for Old Glory.

I was hungry, tired, and confused. The army had drummed into our heads that we should never surrender our ID cards. Behind the faceless window at the terminal, I was told to surrender that very card so they could issue me the necessary "flag orders." Let me tell you that I was damned perplexed. I surrendered my ID, traded a GI for some d-marks (deutsche marks), and brought some food. Off to West Berlin—the Outpost City would never be the same again!

As Lieutenant Sam (as I'll call him) drove onto the autobahn, I suddenly became terrified at the speed of the cars as they drove past us. Lieutenant Sam was going in excess of ninety miles per hour, and BMWs and Mercedes-Benzes were passing by at speeds well in excess of one hundred miles per hour. He laughed at my concern and said, "You'll get used to it. They all drive like this in Germany, and the autobahn has no speed limit." Within a week, I would be studying the international DMV laws and taking the

International Driving Permit test to secure my license. In the usual military wisdom of the times, there was no BOQ (bachelor officers' quarters) available—again, no room at the inn. Really, it's a wonder that we ever won a war. I was put on a waiting list, typical of army protocol. I was assigned to a local guesthouse, where I stayed for the next two weeks as I became acclimated to the military routine of life in the western zone of Germany. In typical army parlance of the Cold War, we referred to West Germany as the "zone."

CHAPTER 5
BEING CONCERNED AT THE KASERNE

*An East German joke about Walter Ulbricht and Willy Brandt,
told during the 1970s (the well-told joke circulated in West
Germany):
"Have you a hobby, Herr Brandt?"
"Yes, I collect jokes that people tell about me," says Brandt.
"And you?"
"Oh, I collect people who tell jokes about me," says Ulbricht.*

The army quite literally sent me down the road on Wurzburger
Strasse and around the bend to a local guesthouse of long-
standing German tradition. The lodgings were typical of
wayside inns scattered throughout Germany. The first floor consisted
of a pub-like restaurant that served local German fare. Along with
the eats, there were the taps for the local beer on draft. As an aside,
it seemed as if every town of consequence had its own brewery, and
in towns with American military presence, they had a cold tap for the
Yankees. The Germans preferred their beer at room temperature. On
the second floor were four rooms for tourists or, as in my case, army
officers in need of shelter. In all its German quaintness, these rooms
shared a single bathroom. My stay at the guesthouse was for a little
over two weeks as I waited for a vacant BOQ.

It was early March of 1970, and the weather was damp with a
trace of snow on the ground. Since I had no means of transportation,
I walked around the bend of Wurzburger Strasse in the early morning

mist of a drab Monday morning. I walked onto Graves Kaserne, which housed the entire First Battalion, Seventh Infantry unit; I was heading to meet Lieutenant Colonel Dillon, the battalion commander. All incoming officers must report formally to the commander, and they have to endure the traditional "Welcome-to-the-greatest-unit-in-the-army" soliloquy. As I listened to my leader's words of wisdom, my mind wondered off in hopes that I could be an effective officer in the execution of my duties. After visiting the S-1 (head of battalion personnel), I was told to report to the commander of headquarters and headquarters company. I was assigned as the Redeye Missile platoon leader.

Getting into the Routine

Throughout my life and in all my endeavors, whether in school or later in life in my career, it has always taken time for me to assimilate and get the lay of the land. My skills of cognition for new procedures and routines are based on observations and hands-on experience. This is the way I learn and recognize my routines, duties, and responsibilities. As I first met my platoon, the routines of a long-standing garrison unit were a mystery to me. One thing that was drilled into our heads in IOBC was that we were to rely on our senior NCOs (noncommissioned officers) or, as in my case, the platoon sergeant. As luck would have it, I ended up with Beetle Bailey with three stripes and a rocker.

Sergeant Bailey was a twelve-year veteran who made the army his career choice; in all honesty, it was likely because he couldn't do anything else. When I asked him what the daily routine was, he showed me the training schedule. In garrison duty throughout my tour of duty in Germany, I found out one indisputable fact: the duty schedule was a worthless piece of paper. So there I was with two worthless things: Sergeant Bailey and a document that in reality meant absolutely nothing. In looking at the schedule for that particular day, I noticed that on that morning, it was designated "Commander's time." I questioned Sergeant Bailey, asking, "What the hell is 'Commander's time'?" His answer still amuses me: "I guess it's time to be used at the discretion of the commander." So you tell me, what was I to do?

On Being an Officer

During the time span that we now call the Vietnam era, junior officers of the line (combat arms of infantry, armor, and artillery) were immediately to possess confidence, knowledge of all facets of their command, and leadership qualities—in the context of a successful junior officer, a large ego with a noted military swagger. When entering a line unit as a junior officer during these times, there was no honeymoon period. The honeymoon ended when we left Fort Bliss.

In looking at the dilemma of my responsibilities as well as how I would conduct myself in this environment, I looked to my fellow officers to see what they would advise in my time of need. Looking at it in the perspective of forty-two years of experience, I would classify the different types of officers prevalent in the Vietnam era based on how one obtained his commission:

Listed below are the officer types that existed in the zone of West Germany in 1970.

1. ROTC officers: This classification was a combination of gung ho career officers who may or may not be competent and the manager-like officer who was competent but just wanted to do his duty and return to civilian life. In other words an officer who wanted to do the job right and go back to the regular civilian existence. This category, as with the other categories, had its share of incompetent officers.

2. OCS officers: This classification was officers who had graduated from Officer Candidate School. For the most part, these officers tended to be enthusiastic. They had worked their way up from the enlisted ranks and were trying to prove themselves in their military leadership roles. As a rule, this group was far more aggressive and tended to be cocky and ever mindful that they had worked their way up the ladder from the enlisted ranks.

3. West Point officers: When speaking of graduates of the United States Military Academy, some people think of officers that are overbearing. In general, I found these

officers to be the best-trained leaders; they were low-key, down-to-earth, and calm under most any circumstances.

On Being a Green Second Lieutenant

My tour of duty in Germany lasted eighteen months, of which I spent fourteen months in a line unit. Of these fourteen months, approximately seven months were spent in garrison duty, and seven months were spent either in the field or at military training facilities. I spent the first couple of months in garrison, where I learned to be an officer of the line the hard way, making mistakes in every possible fashion. I made mistakes of omission, mistakes in trusting the wrong people, and mistakes in attention to detail.

For example, one of the main secondary duties of a junior officer is to perform the duty of "officer of the day" (OD). In a battalion-size unit, this duty takes place approximately once a month in garrison. The officer of the day was in charge of the battalion after duty hours. Along with being in charge, the OD had the supervision of the guard detail who secured the battalion ASP (ammunition supply point). The size of the guard detail was approximately twelve men assigned from each company in the battalion. The duty of the officer of the day was to oversee the entire battalion and be on call should any emergency, such as overseas communications of any family emergencies for any garrisoned soldier.

In addition, if incidents of misconduct or any other disturbances took place, the officer of the day was responsible for addressing them. The officer-of-the-day responsibility ran from 18:00 hours to 06:00 hours. The first and foremost action done by the OD was to inspect the guard detail and name a supernumerary (superior soldier), who would be relieved of guard for excellence of any guard duty. In my greenness of being an OD, I chose a STRAC (a soldier who possesses good military bearing) soldier. Unfortunately, another soldier contested my selection on the basis that the soldier I selected was not in uniform.

Of all things, my selection was missing his med pack, thus putting him out of uniform. Talk about being embarrassed. Indeed, my sin was the lack of attention to detail. So this is what I mean by learning the hard way. In the small world that is battalion army life, word gets around. Here I was, trying to overcome my rookie mistakes among the vultures of combat veteran captains and other aggressive alpha-type first and second lieutenants.

I found out soon enough which officers could walk the walk, and which were devious and couldn't be trusted. As time would show, what one did in the field was what separated the haves from the have-nots. Also, I learned that in Germany, the politics and the games played by the lifers (career officers) were nasty practices based on a non-merit evaluation system predicated on the old "You-scratch-my-back-and-I'll-scratch-yours" mentality.

As I became more experienced in garrison duty, I learned the tricks of the trade. Nine months later, while doing my duties as OD, I took my charge of selecting a supernumerary to the extreme. As I found no one in correct uniform, I selected no one. When I reported my findings to the battalion XO (executive officer), I was told to pick the most in-uniform soldier. With a wink of his eye and a smirk, the XO made it clear that he knew I'd made my point and was no longer a green second lieutenant.

Life at the Kaserne

Life in garrison revolved around duties in the kaserne. All junior officers took their meals at the O-Club and ran up a tab to be paid at the beginning of each month. There was no American TV at the time; the only thing American emanated in the airwaves of West Germany over AFN (Armed Forces Network) radio system. The Special Services ran movie theaters at over a hundred kasernes in West Germany. The fact remains that an individual could rely on everything American and never really know about the German people or their culture. However, this was not my way as I traveled all over Western Europe, including France, Belgium, the Netherlands, and Berlin. Of course, along the way, I always had a cold Yankee (German) beer.

A typical day in the zone was usually a twelve-hour day that started at 05:15 hours and found me hustling to company formation for reveille at 06:00 hours. The mess hall would have breakfast, and by 07:00 hours, our company would be headed to the rifle range to qualify on their M-16 rifle. After my first few times in the field, it was determined that of all the officers in the battalion, I was best qualified to run a range as the range officer. In the running of a rifle range, I was responsible not only for the proper discharge of the weapons but also for accounting for ammunition spent and the proper storage of all unused ammunition. It was also my responsibility to have the area properly policed (cleaned up) and to insure the safety of all present on the range site.

Qualifying a company took all day, and as range officer, I arranged with the mess sergeant to have a hot lunch served adjacent to the range. My goal was to have the last rounds fired downrange by 16:00 hours. After instructing my NCOs to inspect the policing of the range and accounting for spent ammunition and proper cleanup of brass (shell casings collected and recycled by the army), the entire company was given back to the company commander who was responsible for their transport back to the kaserne.

Back at the kaserne, there would be a company formation with the normal duty information and mail call. Usually the company was dismissed at 18:00 hours. The EM (enlisted men) would go to the mess hall for dinner, and most of the bachelor officers would head to the O-Club for dinner. Most of the single officers spent most of the night at the O-Club, playing cards or the slot machines and drinking at the bar.

Getting the Lay of the Land

As time moved forward, garrison duty became routine, and I was more familiar and proficient in the completion of my assigned duties. With my increased confidence, along with my proficiency in my field duties, I was beginning to gain the respect of my peers. As you will see in my saga of field exploits, I will show knowledge along with a stubborn streak of calling it like it is. My superiors shuddered when I displayed my independence in garrison. As I gained a certain swagger of competence, the STRAC big-mouthed junior officers who looked good in barracks became mere insignificant braggarts in the field.

With kasernes like ours scattered throughout Bavaria, the local Germans tolerated our presence as they had done since the end of the war. "Tolerate" is the key word. We were not loved. In the zone, West Germans were beginning to forget what we were there for, and how much we had assisted them in their recovery. Being a proud people, they knew we represented the initial line of defense in the Cold War, but what they really wanted was for our presence to vanish and for a unification of Germany to occur. We troops were but mere pawns in this psychological war, and we were to stay another nineteen years, until the long, hard winter turned into spring.

Chapter 6
A Funny Thing Happened on the Way to the Alert

A Toto Chapter

B erlin: I kept on forgetting that the French and British troops were part of the divided city. This wasn't just an American occupation, it was an Allied agreement negotiated at Potsdam which had an American general in command.

Every month, we had an alert. Some general in US Army European Headquarters would decide to call an alert, usually at 02:00 hours or thereabouts. Units were expected to mobilize to a designated location somewhere in Germany and prepare to defend (in theory) against twenty-one Russian divisions. We were slightly outnumbered.

I was assigned to Berlin Brigade Headquarters, and there was a special alert where we had to coordinate with the Brits and the French. I met a French lieutenant for my liaison. Only problem was that he did not speak English, and my high school French was some seven years rusty. I tried using my schoolbook French. Somehow, we were not making a connection. Then my counterpart realized I was trying to talk to him in French. He'd thought I was speaking German. So much for French II.

The Charge of the Drunken Brigade

Rumor had it that during the 1960s, a US general believed that if the Russians were to attack, they would do so on a weekend or a major US holiday. So this general called an alert at 00:30 hours on New Year's Day. Well, you don't have to be a Rhodes Scholar to guess the outcome. Drunken officers and NCOs scorched the German landscape with APCs, tanks, and "deuce and a half" trucks (two and a half ton rated trucks). Buildings were pummeled, roadways were defaced, and hundreds of trees were uprooted. The damage to the German countryside was several million dollars. This general was immediately reassigned, which just shows that a good idea and liquor don't mix.

Ah, back to the Cold War. My assignments in Berlin were, to say the least, unusual. These alerts were the closest thing to military in field training that I experienced in Berlin. My college training was in business management. Officers' records were screened, and I ended up at brigade headquarters in a study group, and then as the central accounting officer. Not bad for an infantry officer.

Living in the Lap of Luxury

I had a BOQ (bachelor officers' quarters) that most people in the zone could only dream about. I had my own apartment, complete with all utensils, china, and appliances. I soon acquired what everyone in Germany had to have—a state-of-the-art stereo system. I still have the components to this day. American Forces Network was the spot on the dial that most GIs had memorized. There was a nonmilitary radio station, Radio Luxemburg, that broadcast in four languages (Italian, French, German, and English), each for four hours at a time. English was between 20:00 hours and 24:00 hours. On this station, I heard Elton John for the first time. It was during the "Brother John Show."

American Forces Network (AFN) had a tough time trying to entertain the young soldier while placating the "brass" with proper music, including the "1505 to Nashville" (C&W time). And naturally, there were the military commercials. Every day, we would hear radio announcements about reenlisting, or "re-upping." Then there was a series about getting to know your host country, and the announcer would say something like this: "What's the German word for _____?" I thought that the announcer would try to teach us nonmilitary words. But no, AFN brass would never approve something so practical! So we learned the word for tank, (*panzer*) noncommissioned officer (*unter-officer*), and captain (*hauptman*). I tried working those words into a conversation with my German friends, but somehow those subjects never arose.

I had acquired a secondhand black-and-white television. I could receive Armed Forces Network and West and East German television shows. The AFN started at 16:00 on weekdays and 08:00 on weekends. The movies shown were vintage 1940s; however, there was NFL football from the previous week, which was great. There was also the not-so-great. East German television would sometimes air actual films from Vietnam (from their perspective). They repeatedly aired a Vietcong ambush of an American patrol. It still haunts me to this day. You wanted to scream and try to warn them of the ambush. Of course, it was propaganda, but a close-up shot of a dead American soldier's rank and insignia chilled my blood and was a cold shower for my future duties.

Social Tension of the Pre-Volunteer Army

The social/military aspect of Berlin was a microcosm of world events. We had a grand total of one black officer and one female officer in the entire brigade. The black officer was a decent guy, and he became a local hero to many of the young black soldiers who were looking for someone they could identify with. The female officer turned out to be a cool person, single-handedly changing a brigade regulation on travel to East Berlin.

There was no camaraderie between black and white enlisted personnel. The reader should note that we are talking about very young men who were reaching out to identify themselves. And remember that this was a not a volunteer army. The black soldiers developed a ritual of slapping hands, feet, shoulders, and so forth, upon meeting other black soldiers. When the white enlisted personnel copied their ritual, they quickly changed their movements. Then there were the drugs.

Drugs, an Army-Wide Problem

There were "juicers" and "heads." Juicers drank alcohol to excess, and the heads did drugs. The drug of choice was hashish. There was Lebanese Red, Afghan Black, and Mary Jane (marijuana), of course. Heroin was "horse" or "scag." I did not encounter heroin in Germany, but Vietnam was another issue. Believe it or not, I did not take drugs. I had enough to deal with, as the officers' happy hour (from 17:00 to 19:00 hours) meant twenty-five cents for top-shelf liquor and fifteen cents for imported beer. For two dollars, you could get wasted. One time during a Chicago concert, a fan next to me asked me to please (*bitte*) pass something along; it turned out to be hashish pipe, and I was certain I would be arrested. Another confrontation averted.

While I did not participate in drugs, I did not bust anyone who may have shared his confidence with me. When I had officer-of-the-day duties, I would pound on the front entrance to the barracks and shout loudly, "Officer of the day coming through!" Then I would give those soldiers two minutes to stop whatever they were doing. If they continued to do drugs, I would bust them. Also, if I even smelled the aroma of marijuana on duty, hell was to be paid.

While I was in Berlin, President Nixon had allowed the military to enter Cambodia. True to their Western counterparts, groups of students protested in front of Berlin Brigade Headquarters. We were not allowed to participate in any demonstration. Our opinions were shared only with closest friends.

Berlin: A Haven for a Bachelor

Berlin was fantastic for a young bachelor lieutenant. One of the anomalies of WWII German male deaths was an overabundance of females. There was a nightclub called Café Kaiser, where the women asked the men to dance. If the male refused to dance with two or three women, he was asked to leave. The Berlin woman became aggressive in their pursuit of men. It was commonplace for a twenty-four-year-old woman to marry a man in his fifties. I was twenty-three, and a particular woman in her forties, who was much taller than I, was somehow enamored with my charisma. But I am not complaining; it was a great time.

We bachelors, true to our levels of testosterone, were determined to meet as many females as we could, especially American tourists. We had stumbled upon the itinerary of an eight-week tour group of Europe. These charming recent college graduates first landed in Frankfurt and then spent the next two weeks in non-English-speaking countries (Poland, Czechoslovakia, Russia, and so on). On consecutive Mondays, a busload of young women would enter one of a chain of nightclubs, and we were ready to greet them with our English salutations. They eagerly jumped at the chance of talking with Americans.

Some of the encounters led to serious relationships, with women actually leaving the tour group and spending two to three weeks with their new heartthrobs. It was commonplace during the summer months for a young bachelor's phone to ring at 01:00 hours, with a plea from the caller to run to his BOQ because he had four extra girls. No wonder I was always tired.

The social climate was great, but it was not like the United States. At the entrance to some clubs, one rang a bell and then was eyeballed by a German who had opened a peephole in the door, reminiscent of the speakeasies of the 1920s. If he didn't like the way you looked, dressed, or talked, you were not allowed in, period. We had many challenges in entering the most popular German clubs. I eventually made some German friends from the Free University in Berlin. We accompanied them to clubs, and after the passage of time the clubs' gatekeepers recognized us. After a few months, we were considered okay.

One club continued to be a challenge. Neither my friends nor I had any luck getting in. As I previously mentioned, one of my duties was that of central accounting officer. I managed twelve civilians, six of whom were German citizens. This accounting office was responsible for the finances of four enlisted clubs, one NCO club and one officers' club. I asked one of the German workers if she could find out anything about this club. Within a few days, she had information for me: "Oh, Lieutenant, you don't want to go into that club … It is not for you." It turned out that only gays and lesbians frequented the club. No wonder we couldn't gain entry.

We did our best to blend in with the local populace. Unfortunately, our haircuts and our clothing were dead giveaways. My new German friends introduced me to the game of soccer. I had played the game once at a children's summer camp but didn't know some of the rules. They took me to a number of games, which I truly enjoyed. My circle of friends expanded significantly.

The Lieutenant with Chicken Pox

One of my new friends was married and had a son named Stephan. He was about three years old and cute as a button. I tried to learn as much German as I could so I could communicate with him. Little did I know that would bring me grief. Turns out, he gave me the chicken pox.

I was feeling lousy one weekend, just after having visited Stephan. I woke up on Monday and started to shave. As I looked in the mirror, I saw blotches everywhere. I dressed and reported for sick call. There was a long line of soldiers waiting to be seen, and people suddenly started stepping aside for me until I was at the front of the line. I must have looked worse than I thought.

After examining me, a doctor asked if he could bring in another doctor—I was starting to be concerned. They conferred with one another and with drawings in a medical book. Then I was told that I probably had the chicken pox, but I had recently received a booster for smallpox, and they were going to quarantine me for twenty-four hours to be positive I didn't have smallpox. The sight of bubbly pox the next morning confirmed a diagnosis of chicken pox. I still had to be quarantined—but only to my BOQ for two weeks. My friends brought me food, which they left at the door. I felt like a leper. So much for my social life.

CHAPTER 7
OUT IN THE FIELDS

W ildflecken, early May 1970:

The flag is up! The flag is waving! The flag is down! Targets up! Lock and load one magazine—twenty rounds! Are you ready on the right? The right is ready! Are you ready on the left? The left is ready! The firing line is ready! Commence firing!

The above was the actual protocol I used in running an M-16 KD (known distance) rifle range. I would run this range for a period of three days when my CO (commanding officer) ordered me to run the M-60 machine gun range. In the field, the schedule extended to seven days. On the seventh day (Sunday), there was chaplain's time and commander's time, which usually meant the cleaning of weapons and vehicles. Wildflecken was an old Wehrmacht training center located in Bavaria, in the district of Bad Kissingen. The US Army had control of Camp Wildflecken since April 1945. It was originally utilized as a displaced persons housing camp from 1945 to 1951. After 1951, Wildflecken was used as the Seventh Army training center under the auspices of the Training Command of Grafenwoehr.

Lieutenant Geschke as range officer
Wildflecken, 1970

In the realm of zone training, the mere mention of Grafenwoehr conjured visions of the training of SS units and panzer armored commands inspired by the essence of the Thousand-Year Reich. In reality, training in the zone was serious and thorough. Mistakes were not tolerated, and many an OER (officer efficiency report) was mindful of what one did or did not do in the field. The protocol was quite straightforward and tolerated no made-up stories. It was either put up or shut up!

Establishing a Reputation

As my CO instructed me during the second week in Wildflecken how to run the APC (armored personnel carrier) .50-caliber machine gun range, I began to wonder why the West Point officers weren't called to the task. They were the professionals, weren't they? How could an ROTC lieutenant be running the complicated tasks of an APC .50-caliber machine gun range? Somehow, I seemed to have developed a niche with a command presence, albeit based on bravado and the hope that I wouldn't screw up. In fact, I had one APC .50-caliber machine gun fail to fire due to improper headspace and timing. Far from being an expert, I called in my range NCO to fix the problem, which he quickly and efficiently did. I closely looked at the procedure performed by my NCO, mentally noted the fix, and smartly moved on. In the eyes of all concerned, I was a lieutenant who was knowledgeable and commanded respect.

On those ranges in Wildflecken, I was able to shake off my second-lieutenant greenness and show that I was able to perform in the field. My peers were beginning to believe, but my total acceptance still waited in abeyance.

Into the Thick of It!

Graves Kaserne, Aschaffenburg, June 1970:

We left the field to go back to the usual boring garrison life in A'Burg. Although this time, things were not so boring, and activity and excitement reigned supreme through all of Graves Kaserne. We were put on a Seventh Army alert to Jordan. Since this was my first experience of a unit alert, I learned how fast a unit could get packed and ready to deploy to a faraway land. In a matter of eighteen hours, our unit was loaded and ready to go—lock, stock, and barrel—with all equipment and weapons operational. Once we were ready, we waited and waited … and waited some more. Three days later, orders were given to stand down. So much for exciting travel and adventures! We were all dressed and ready with no place to go—well, not really no place; there was that land in which Hitler's panzers trained, and it was nestled in the pine barrens of Upper Palatinate Bavaria. This was life in a line unit in Germany during the Vietnam era.

Lieutenant Geschke during Jordan alert
Graves Kaserne, June 1970

Packed and ready to go for Jordan Alert
Graves Kaserne, June 1970

Training in Hitler's Playground

Grafenwohr, July 1970:

The summers in West Germany were temperate and comfortable, with hardly any humidity or hot days. There was only one place in the FRG (Federal Repulic of Germany) in which this idyllic summer weather was an oxymoron, and that location was a major training area by the name of Grafenwoehr, or as we lovingly dubbed it, "Graf." To this day, the United States Army operates the military training facility of over ninety square miles in Grafenwoehr, Germany. The first artillery round was fired at Grafenwoehr by a German battery at 08:00 hours on June 30, 1910. Since then, the land has been used for the training of military line units. The terrain in Grafenwoehr during the summer reminded me of a gigantic dustbowl contained by a forested land of conifers, much like the pine barrens of Long Island. The dust was created by the constant wear and tear on the soil by such track vehicles as APCs and tanks. During heavy rains, the land was nothing but a large mud field, known to throw track vehicles into disrepair. In fair weather, walking about the fields of Graf was like being Pig Pen of *Peanuts* lore. In the zone during the Cold War, the use of the combined arms of infantry and armor was like the cartoon team of Yogi and Boo Boo.

In the summer of 1970, Grafenwoehr was nothing but a cloud of dust amid the pine barrens of northern Bavaria, with tanks and APCs effectively perfecting their maneuvers of traversing in reverse with their guns pointed east in order to deter a Warsaw Pact attack. In all my field duty in West Germany, one irrevocable picture I have in my mind is of M-60 tanks and M113A1 APCs going in reverse with the guns pointed at the evacuated terrain. Track drivers in the FRG were more proficient driving in reverse than driving forward. Such were the tactics and strategy for all combat units of the line in the US Seventh Army, whose insignia and motto were labeled SEVEN STEPS TO HELL. The primary mission of the Seventh Army was to fight a delaying action against the Warsaw Pact. Our forces were outnumbered at least six to one. In essence, we were mere fodder and pawns in the grand Cold War strategy.

The purpose of this first visit to Graf was the training of my

Redeye Missile platoon during Third Brigade combined arms field maneuvers. My mission was to place my platoon in a position to cover a determined sector to defend the airways of where my company was operating. Utilizing six jeeps (quarter-ton vehicles) with trailers to carry the trainer Redeye Missiles, we set up shop with communications both to battalion headquarters and our FAC (forward air controller). It was our responsibility to coordinate air traffic maneuvers with the FAC. The FAC also provided a total air defense early warning system. The FAC was essentially responsible for reporting all air movements in our area. We were participating in a week's field training exercise that demanded constant attention to detail along with our exposure to the elements of rain and local dust storms caused by the whirlwind of constant flow of track vehicles in the dried mud banks.

Our mission was not a static situation; we were constantly on the move. The keys to success were constant communication and the ability to land navigate under field conditions. Our mission took us through towns that were simple to find when reading a map. However, it was in the open field among the pine barrens and low saddle hills where land navigation and the ability to read a topographical map were necessary skills. In the days before GPS, if you learned one skill as a line officer, it must be the ability to land navigate and read a map not only during the daylight hours but also in night operations or blackout conditions. I was fortunate in my initial FTX (field training exercise); I never got lost, and I was always where I should be. Thus my first FTX at Graf was a success.

Lieutenant Geschke outside Grafenwoehr
Summer 1970

Damned If It Isn't T. Couch!

Coming off the fields of Graf, I remember two things. One, as usual, we exited the fields of Graf at breakneck speed, going in reverse. I can still see the cloud of dirt spewing toward the just traveled area, along with the deafening sounds of metal against metal as the tracks revolved at a high level of rotation. The second thing was Tom Couch visiting Graf in his capacity as the Third Infantry Division PIO (public information officer). Typical Couch in a nice clean uniform and me in my dirty field fatigues—go figure! Life in Germany took on a new meaning for T. Couch. Later we went to the Graf O-Club and belted down a few cold ones. Of course, Couch gave me the lay of the land as to his duties at division headquarters in Wurzburg. Life in the field had a different connotation for T. Couch.

Lieutenant Geschke
Grafenwoehr, Summer 1970

Searching for Recognition

EIB Training, Federal Republic of Germany, Summer 1970:

If you were a soldier of the line in an infantry battalion in the zone, you were required to test for the Expert Infantryman's Badge (EIB). The only line unit personnel exempt from participation were soldiers whose MOS (military occupational specialty) was not infantry, those who already had the EIB, and soldiers who possessed the CIB (Combat Infantryman's Badge). Recipients of the CIB were soldiers who had heard the sounds of guns in an infantry unit in combat.

The process of the EIB training and testing was a long and arduous task. Training started in late May of 1970, in garrison, and extended throughout the summer, both in garrison and in the field, where all the testing was done in Wildflecken. Instructors possessed EIBs or CIBs and were very demanding. Of the over 180 participants in the EIB program, only eleven soldiers were awarded the coveted

EIB. During the Vietnam era of the 1960s and 1970s, approximately fifteen stations had to be passed in the final examination, which ranged from the subjects of clearing a mine and setting a claymore to qualifying with a rifle and calling in artillery.

The Problems of Land Navigation

A prime example to show the great degree of difficulty a soldier encounters in the pursuit of the EIB, one need look no further than the land navigation station. In 1970, there was no such thing as GPS. A soldier was expected to know how to read a map, and these maps were not your everyday road maps. A soldier had to know how to read a military topographical map. Most of the times in the field, one was not even close to a road. By having the ability to identify use of contour lines and elevation marks, one could ascertain where one was. Being able to read a map in the field was important; however, along with this knowledge, one also had to know how to navigate with a magnetic compass. This took constant practice, and the way to improve was to constantly train out in the field. To do this effectively, we practiced by searching for markers placed in the field. Once you became proficient in doing this, the army threw you a curve and demanded that a soldier had to do this in night maneuvers.

Doing land navigation on foot becomes second nature. However, if you're in a mechanized infantry unit, land navigation becomes accelerated at, shall we say, "warp speed." Try finding markers going at thirty-five miles per hour over rough terrain on tracked vehicles in fifteen-degree weather and the wind chill at below zero. Luckily, for the EIB test, we were required to hit the markers in full daylight. In this EIB training, I was fortunate enough to max out on all my markers and score perfectly. Even before taking this battery of tests, the soldier had to complete a timed forced march with full field gear. Also, the soldier had to pass the army physical proficiency test with a score of over seventy-five. EIB training for the required testing of the fifteen stations was done both in garrison and under actual field conditions. Hands-on training was required in order to be successful in the pursuit of the EIB.

It's Not Easy!

If the soldier qualified on the forced march and the physical proficiency test, he was to be included in the final EIB testing of the fifteen stations located in Wildflecken. The testers were known not to give any quarter to any EIB candidate. To receive the EIB, the candidate had to pass all fifteen tests to qualify. Under the rules of the EIB at that time, a candidate could fail three of fifteen tests and qualify for a retest. If the candidate passed the retest, which was only given one time, the candidate would receive the EIB. This scenario was a long and grueling process that required study, dedication, and an attitude that there was no fear of failure. As luck would have it, I passed fourteen of fifteen stations on my initial attempt at Wildflecken in August 1970. The only station that I failed was the clearing of a mine area.

We only had one soldier who passed all fifteen tests, and he was a first lieutenant who was a West Point graduate. I immediately sought his counsel as to how to pass this last station. This particular test required patience utilizing a blade of a knife to gently detect where the mine was hidden. Once the mine was located, I had a complicated protocol in which engineers would mark and subsequently disarm the mine. He helped me with fulfilling these requirements as I retested at Wildflecken a week later. With the help of my West Point friend, I passed the final station.

Two weeks later at a battalion formation, the eleven candidates were awarded their EIBs. At least my field exploits were washing away my inexperience. To me, training in the field was challenging and much more relevant than playing politics in garrison.

CHAPTER 8
WEST BERLIN: DIVISIONS OF CITY AND COUNTRY

A Toto Chapter

I had no idea what I would encounter when I finished my trip on board the duty train.

I arrived at 07:00 hours at the train station in West Berlin, having traveled all night from Frankfurt. I was not aware of the changing of the locomotives at East Germany, nor of the same at East Berlin. I was tired, hungry, and dirty. As I awaited the presence of olive green at the station, I was greeted by the S-1 (administrative) of the Third Battalion, Sixth Infantry. Since my orders were for a different battalion, I was confused. "You were transferred from the Four Eighteen," said the captain. "Let's load your belongings into my car."

I was to learn that I would be assistant S-4 (supply) because I was "surplus," the result of too many lieutenants signing on for "voluntary indefinite." I did reports of surveys, the equivalent of "whom to blame for military losses," for two months, before I was transferred to brigade headquarters.

I became enamored with the history of Berlin. I read everything I could about the divided city—four sectors, according to the Potsdam Agreement: Spandau (England), Wedding (French), the American sector, and East Berlin (Russian). I was ashamed at my lack of knowledge of Berlin history.

The evidence of the political situation was everywhere. There were West German d'marks and East German d'marks. The conversion rate was one dollar to three and a half d'marks, and then four East German d'marks to one West German d'mark. Buying in East Berlin was the equivalent of 75 percent off via Home Shopping Network. Most of all, there was "the wall."

The Iron Curtain Unplugged

The wall consisted of sections of concrete protected by tank traps, minefields, East German guards, and a labyrinth of obstacles which was used as a barrier to East Germans seeking refuge in West Berlin. I saw the wall before the graffiti scorched the borders … the cold gray fence preventing the East Berliners from touching their relatives and embracing their heritage. Scaffolds were built on the west side that rose above the wall so people could see the visions beyond the wall.

Sometimes there were families gathering upon the deck so they could wave to relatives clear of the wall and send kisses to the trapped prisoners of the USSR. It was about sadness and the spirit of the human being … something the wall could not suppress. It was about courage and the will to survive as a free person. It was beautiful but sometimes deadly. As FDR said, "I hate war," but he was not around to see the Cold War and the Iron Curtain.

The division of four sectors and the building of the wall made for architectural anomalies. Some homes were splintered by the demarcation lines, resulting in a facade pressed into the wall. There were remnants of subway stations, with only a sign as proof of their existence. There were crazy angles to the paved streets, following precisely the agreed-upon boundaries. Even the wall itself was not uniform. In the French sector (Wedding), parts of the old wall had yet to be renovated. On top of the wall, the flat surface was embedded with broken glass so that escapees would cut their hands as they tried to climb over the wall. Also, there were strands of barbed wire anchored with triangular posts. The Russians had tried to improve their image by replacing most of the glass and barbed wire with a circular aluminum pipe. This replacement looked less menacing but their real purpose was to have grappling hooks slip off the aluminum surface. Then there were the historical treasures.

Berlin, 1970

Berlin Wall in foreground
East Berlin in background

The Presence of the Russian Bear

Perhaps by accident, most of the historical treasures of Berlin were isolated behind the wall. Opera houses, museums, art treasures, and prominent buildings were now in East Berlin. It is no secret that the Germans feared the Russians, and the Russians could not forget the Battle of Moscow. There was a Russian cemetery built on the outskirts of East Berlin, dedicated to the Russian soldiers who were killed during the invasion of Berlin in World War II. Ten thousand Russian soldiers were interred standing up, with their shoulders touching their comrades, facing due east toward Moscow.

The Russians used German prisoners around the clock for twelve months to build the wonderful expanse. The cemetery entrance was constructed of an archway made of red marble confiscated from Hitler's bunker (Führerbunker), which was destroyed by the Russian troops.

Upon entering the cemetery, I was awestruck by a statue of Mother Russia facing north over the gravesites of the Russian soldiers who were killed. The gravesites were landscaped with marble walkways and various assortments of flowers. The statue is a soldier holding a baby, which signifies Germany, while crushing a swastika under his boot. Inside the archway, under the statue, are mosaics of peasant workers. Their faces are looking to the center of the chamber, where a book containing the names of the dead soldiers buried there is placed on a lectern. Very moving and a place that most West Berliners didn't even know existed.

Living in West Berlin at that time is difficult to describe. The West Berliners loved the American military presence and feared the Russians. Perhaps it best described by attempting to talk first about East Berlin.

We were allowed to travel into East Berlin, but only in uniform and during daylight hours. I enjoyed shopping in little-known shops for crystal and "communist" articles—busts of Marx and flags from the communist countries (North Korea, USSR, and so on). East Berlin had 2.5 million people yet only two gas stations. Lines of people queued up at every basic store for bread, eggs, milk, and other staples.

There were huge throngs of people walking in the marketplace, but no one was talking to other people. Their clothes were seasonable but lacking in color. They wore drab gray, black, dark green, and dark brown. When someone in a US uniform was spotted, you'd catch a glimpse of a stranger rushing to a pay phone—our location was being communicated to the "state."

Thank God for the children. We always carried gum, candy, and other treats when we travelled to the "East." Children would crowd around us, led on by a sense of curiosity and desire. They eagerly accepted our donations and thanked us in basic German. We only stayed for a few hours at a time.

A War of Fear and Nerves

Back in West Berlin, we had only to walk near the wall during the summertime to understand freedom. You would hear gunshots coming from the East and read about another escape foiled by the East Berlin police. Or you could stroll by the river and see the armed Russian/East German patrol boats in their round-the-clock cruising. You could visit "Checkpoint Charlie," the entry point to the East, and visit the Mauermuseum nearby. This museum is better known to all GIs as the "escape museum." The Cold War was all around us.

Checkpoint Charlie, 1970

We had a bevy of international intelligence and counterintelligence. We had Radio Free Europe, whose signals were jammed by the state every day. We had "mission" duty, which was to be pulled by a different officer every day. It consisted of riding in a mission car, which was a gray high-horsepower monster with bulletproof glass and a fifty-gallon gas tank. We had to travel on a certain road to Potsdam, the site of the WWII agreement, to keep our rights open to this passageway.

It was the same rationale for having three air corridors into West Berlin as well as the duty trains that left Bremerhaven, West Berlin, and Frankfurt. All these avenues of entry and exit kept Berlin in contact with Western Europe. These were the same air corridors that flew 24/7 during the Berlin Airlift to save the city of West Berlin. Several military personnel were killed during that military operation. The people of West Berlin would never forget either that or JFK's speech before the Brandenburg Gate.

East Berlin was dark, dusky, and silent. That is not how it felt in the West, where I was comfortable walking down Ku'damm at 01:00 hours without fearing for my life.

Our brigade motto was "Defenders of Freedom." I learned

something about that motto during my tour of West Berlin. And I almost wept when the wall finally came down. God bless America!

Bombed out WWII East Berlin Building in background
Berlin Wall in foreground, 1970

CHAPTER 9
ICH BIN EIN BERLINER
(I AM A JELLY DOUGHNUT)

A Toto Chapter

As previously mentioned, I did not have the typical duties of an infantry lieutenant. I began my trek to brigade headquarters as part of a study group consisting of one major, two captains, and two lieutenants, with me being junior. Guess who got all the extra duties. Without going into exact details of our mission (because some details may be still classified), I will divulge that we were to point out areas in the budget that could be eliminated if Berlin Brigade resources were reduced.

The major reported directly to the commanding general, General Berry, who was one of the finest people I have ever met, military or civilian. We pored over mission statements, operations plans, and so forth, in order to make the proper recommendations. The people we interviewed, especially the intelligence community, looked upon us with some suspicion.

Remember, we had all kinds of political establishments in Berlin. "Spooks," as we called the intelligence/counterintelligence operatives, had military and political missions, and they were not too happy with any challenges to their operations. I spent nine months in the study group, and my name was known to the brass because of our duties.

At the end of the assignment, I was returned to the S-4 shop at the Infantry Battalion Third of the Sixth.

Looking for a Line Unit

I was a first lieutenant by then, still dumb but with some knowledge. I had been in Berlin for over a year, and I just knew that the time would come shortly for my return to the infantry. I had not served in a line unit, and I requested an audience with the battalion commander to ask for an assignment. I explained that I would probably be ordered to Vietnam shortly and had no line experience. He listened politely and assigned me to a Redeye Missile platoon, starting one week from that day.

The next day, I received a phone call from a major at brigade headquarters, offering me a position of some secrecy. I politely refused, stating my reasons (my lack of line experience). He thanked me and hung up. Within two hours, I was called to report to the battalion commander. When I arrived, he started to berate me about talking to a major in the brigade about an assignment. I assured him that I had not initiated the inquiry and had declined the offer, telling him that I was excited about my new assignment in his battalion.

The next morning, I was told to report to the assistant brigade commander, a full colonel in the infantry. He asked me why I had declined the assignment at brigade headquarters, and I repeated the above statements. He thanked me, and I left. Within two hours, I received another call from the battalion commander, telling me to report to the commanding general by 12:00 hours; he thanked me for my loyalty to the battalion.

I reported to the commanding general, a man I truly respected. Outside of his office, his aide, a friend of mine from West Point, announced my arrival. I asked him what was going on, and he said, "I don't know, Bob."

General Berry was a physically imposing man and a great leader. I would have done anything for him, and I think that he knew it. Upon my reporting, he said, "Toto, how stupid do you think our military is? I've heard your reasons for turning down this assignment. Do you truly think that a commander in a war zone would turn over a platoon of men to a lieutenant with no troop experience? But I'll leave it up to you; if you decline this assignment, I will honor your wishes. Please know that I need you for this assignment."

I said, "Sir, no commanding officer in a war zone would assign me to a line unit if he could possibly avoid it. If you need me for this assignment, then I will eagerly accept it." He thanked me and told me to report to a major for briefing.

Special Assignment

During this time, there was a major scandal in Vietnam, involving the highest-ranking NCO in Vietnam, Sergeant Major Woolridge (the first sergeant major in the US Army); units were implicated in a major PX, commissar, supply scandal. General Berry was concerned about his unit. My duties were to "look into" any anomalies within the supply system. My investigation lasted about three months. At the conclusion of it, charges were made against three individuals, and one CWO3 (chief warrant officer third grade) was detained, not allowed to retire until another investigation was made. After my assignment ended, I was given a new one: the brigade central accounting officer. By then, my name was known throughout the brigade—not bad for a first lieutenant.

So I began my assignment as the central accounting officer. My group did the inventory control, payroll, personnel actions, and detail accounting for all the service clubs (enlisted, NCO, officer) in the brigade. This also included profit and loss statements for each club, including the slot machines, which were legal at that time. Unbelievably, the membership list to the officers' club was classified—the result of the many "spooks" that were assigned to West Berlin.

As part of my duties, I had to visit these same service clubs unannounced so I could observe whether proper procedures were being followed, such as liquor accountability. Normally, officers are not allowed in enlisted and NCO clubs. The supervisory personnel recognized me and immediately offered a drink. I declined until my audit was complete. Here again, my name was known to another group of soldiers. Incidentally, I paid for all my own drinks, except those bought by officers who outranked me. Geschke never bought me a drink.

Being Social in the Outpost City

It was never all work and no play. Our unit had a "hi/bye" social every month, where we welcomed the new guys and said good-bye to those leaving for duties elsewhere. All officers were expected to be there, regardless of any prior commitments. There were also other socials where our attendance was expected.

Upon arriving in Berlin, I was invited to the general's home for a welcome. The protocol called for us being there for fifteen to twenty minutes and then leaving. The West Pointers and regular army officers left their "calling cards" at the social. Because I did not have any cards, my attendance was not recorded. I was invited to two more socials before General Berry said to me, "Toto, you are here again?"

I said, "Sir, I have no calling cards."

He told me not to worry about not having a card.

We also had a quarterly ball, where we dressed in formal military attire and listened to the lively tunes from the Berlin Brigade Army Band. What a thrill! The Junior Officer Council had requested that this ball not be a command performance. The brass vetoed that. So the company-grade officers devised a plan to "free" us from this bondage.

A number of lieutenants and captains went to the strasse and hired prostitutes to accompany them to the ball. You can imagine how they fit in. They wore all kinds of provocative clothing to the event, much to the dismay of the older army wives. Some wore fishnet dresses without any undergarments, leaving nothing to the imagination. The next week, the Junior Officer Council was informed that the next military ball was to be optional. I never attended another ball.

During the summer, especially during the month of August, most Europeans were on holiday (vacation). Berlin Brigade had a history of participating in an American-German Festival during August. For the two summers that I was in Berlin, the theme was "The American West." Backdrops, German-American flags, and eateries of all types were constructed for the event, as were amusement park rides and games. With my association at the officers' club, I was "volunteered" to work at the taco stand. It turned out to be an enjoyable time. Germans did not have a clue what a taco was, and they eagerly shelled out one mark to try one. They were not disappointed.

Also, the Germans (and most other Europeans) considered corn to be "pig food." They were pleasantly surprised when they ate corn on the cob from the stand. They remarked how good it was, and they could be seen returning to the stand every thirty minutes or so. I learned that "ona ice" meant without ice in the soft drinks. My partner at the stand was a dependent of a military family and had spent several years in Germany. An "army brat," she was a good person and spoke German fluently—I was jealous. I think that military brats get a bum rap. The ones that I met, and sometimes dated, were nice people. They didn't have attitudes, and they truly appreciated the little things that life has to offer.

Berlin is high on the latitude line; the winter daylight hours were short and the summer hours long. A summer day could be eighteen hours of daylight. The temperature never rose above eighty-two or so in the summer, but the winter temperatures could be brutal. Thank God for my German-made Volkswagen; it got me through many a horrible day.

We even had a golf course in Berlin. It's the only course I ever played that had a front ten and a back eight. But golf was extremely cheap. It cost us twenty-five dollars for an entire season of golf. I was never very good at the game, but it was a great escape, and I met different people on the golf course, including lots of brass.

I had made another friend, Bill Haehn from Pennsylvania. A recon platoon leader from Third of the Sixth, he was an expert on the Civil War. He was also airborne/ranger. Why we connected, I'll never know. He took me to places along the wall that even the average military person had never seen. He was a good soldier but a bad budget manager. I lent him the same twenty dollars every month from my paycheck. He also had a Triumph sports car.

Bill had graduated from OCS, immediately escaped from Ft. Benning, and bought a car from the lechers surrounding the post. The car had a bad electrical system and caught on fire before Bill shipped the car to Germany. By the time it arrived in Berlin, Bill didn't know if the car would ever run. It did run, and it was perfect for the small roads in Berlin. Bill awaited orders for Vietnam, as I did, but he received orders for Korea. I have lost contact with Bill over the years but understand that he met a Korean girl while on his assignment, and that he'd been making arrangements to have her brought to the States for marriage. I wish them all my best.

JFK Goofed!

At the beginning of this chapter, I wrote, "I am a jelly doughnut." Grammatically, JFK should have said, "Ich bin Berliner," I am a Berliner. My maid at my BOQ had lunch with me one day and offered me a "Berliner kugler," a jelly doughnut covered in chocolate icing. It was great. So was JFK when he said he was a "jelly doughnut." To the Berliners, he was a savior and a hero, just as General Clay was during the Berlin Airlift. They have a street named after Clay, and a people named after JFK. If the reader has a chance to listen to his speech from June of 1963, please do so, gauging the cheers of the Berliners. It still causes my neck hair to rise when JFK says, "They say that communism is the wave of the future. To them I say, 'Come to Berlin.'" I was privileged to be stationed in Berlin.

CHAPTER 10
ZINGERS IN THE ZONE

Four Dead in Ohio, May 1970

O ccasionally, the subject of where I graduated from college was brought up. When I informed the person that I graduated from Kent State University, he or she would immediately look at me, likely ascertaining that I was of a certain age, and say, "Oh, you were at Kent State when the shootings happened." The answer is a simple no. I graduated from Kent State University in August of 1969, and along with receiving my degree, I was also commissioned a second lieutenant in the US Army Reserve as an infantry officer. The tragic shootings at Kent State took place on May 4, 1970. On that particular day, I was in garrison at Graves Kaserne in Aschaffenburg, Germany. When I heard what transpired, I couldn't believe it. The initial reports would have everyone believing that Kent State was a hotbed of war protestors inundated with long-haired hippies and pot-smoking students.

While it is true that every campus had protestors, and that some students imbibed in smoking weed, the thought of Kent State being a hotbed of protest couldn't be further from the truth. Kent, Ohio, is an idyllic small town located southeast of Cleveland and almost due east from Akron. The university had been in existence for sixty years when the tragedy occurred. The university is known for its excellent college of education and fine arts, especially in the discipline of journalism. The students attending the state university were mostly from the middle classes of northeast Ohio. Its reputation was good, and it reflected the positive aspects of life in the region.

During this time span in American history, the protest movement about our participation in the war in Vietnam was widespread throughout the United States. Lieutenant Calley was about to go to trial at Ft. Benning for the My Lai Massacre, and President Nixon had decided to escalate the war in Vietnam by invading the NVA (North Vietnamese Army) sanctuaries in Cambodia. It was at this point that the SDS (Students for a Democratic Society) became more vocal and active on all campuses in the United States.

Kent State was not spared these actions, and with outside SDS agitation, protests started in the city of Kent proper, not at the university. Protests and destruction of property in the town escalated and moved onto the campus. By May 2, 1970, the ROTC military science building was set ablaze. Things were beginning to get out of control in a hurry. Governor Rhodes called in the Ohio National Guard, who, as it turned out, was ill prepared to handle this escalating riot situation. On May 4, 1970, someone in a leadership position in the National Guard gave the order to fire their M-1 rifles. The tragic results were that four people died. In effect, once those rounds were fired downhill, the war in Vietnam was no longer just a protest; as a result, it started the final movement to end the war in Southeast Asia.

Of course, as a young second lieutenant in Aschaffenburg, Germany, those events came to me in fragmentary newspaper articles that would, of course, be analyzed and studied for everyone to understand in the coming years. The truth and reasons of what happened at Kent State University would take years to unravel. However, to my fellow officer peers, it was another strike against a green second lieutenant who got his commission at that "hippie university."

A Toto Moment

As Dick mentioned, the universities became a focal point for campus unrest. I was in ROTC (Reserve Officers' Training Corps) at Northeastern University in Boston. I was near Harvard and MIT. Wearing a uniform in the 1960s was akin to having a bull's-eye on your back. One day we were marching to a park located in the Fens, where Fenway Park got its name. I was in full uniform and noticed that the student "pacifiers" had climbed some trees in the park and proceeded to throw stones at their classmates—so much for a peaceful demonstration. We had campus sit-ins and all kinds of speeches. Trying to maneuver around campus was equivalent to moving about a zoo.

Students had blockaded the ROTC building and the science building; since Dow Chemical, the maker of napalm, had made a grant to the school, the protesters figured that they were fair targets. After a while, we figured that the instigators of this unrest were people brought in from the outside by the SDS. Unlike past leaders of protest like Saul Alinski, these people used scare tactics to the extreme. When Richard Daley was the mayor, Saul Alinksi was head of a union group of airline workers in Chicago. He planned a "shit-in" at O'Hare International Airport. His plan was to have airline workers occupy every toilet at the airport so that when passengers came off planes, they could not utilize the facilities. Daley found out about the plan one half hour beforehand, and the city renegotiated with the union. Drastic, yes, but no one was hurt. Buildings were not destroyed, and flags were not desecrated. There were several splinter groups, some of which were racially motivated.

Maybe the Vietnam War was wrong, but the soldiers did not make the policy. Trying to tell someone who lost a friend in a firefight that he was a warmonger and part of an illegal establishment was not the place to go. I remember being discharged from active duty and strongly advised not to wear the uniform. What did I do wrong?

The concept that was fertilized by JFK and expanded by LBJ was coming to a screeching halt with "Tricky Dick." Little did we know that the theory of "falling dominoes" had nothing at all to do with either the spread or the stopping of communism. Fourteen years after the fall of Saigon, the wall came tumbling down in Europe, and communism no longer existed in Eastern Europe.

A Payroll Officer, by the Book, 1970–1971

Can you hear it? Tell me you hear it! It's the theme and background music from the movie *Jaws*. This is how every young lieutenant, whether in West Germany, CONUS (Continental US), or anywhere there was a US Army payroll disbursed felt in performing the duties of payroll officer. The most dreaded secondary duty to perform was that of the payroll officer. In my army career, I performed this tortuous duty three times. I did it twice as an officer of the line in A'Burg with the First Battalion, Seventh Infantry. Later I did this duty at Headquarters Company, Third Infantry Division, at Leighton Barracks in Wurzburg, Germany.

In most instances, there was one pay officer for each line company and headquarters company. This duty was duly rotated among all second and first lieutenants. Each lieutenant was assigned an NCO (noncommissioned officer) of E-5 rank or higher. Both the payroll officer and NCO were provided with loaded .45-caliber pistols for their protection while performing the duties of administering the payroll. The standard operating procedures for the payroll officer included reporting to the finance office to procure the pay vouchers and the cash. During this period of military history, all payrolls were done on a cash basis. I was given a cash figure that I counted out not once but twice to assure accuracy.

As required by army regulation, I was required to sign for all the said vouchers and cash. I would proceed to my company's dayroom and set up a table with the vouchers in alphabetical order and my cash spread on the table, categorized by denomination. Once everything was set, the payroll would be disbursed, and the process of paying the troops would continue until 16:30 hours. Each soldier, regardless of rank, would salute and state his rank and name with the phrase "Reporting for pay" at the end of the report. The pay officer would return the salute, locate the voucher, proceed to count the cash, and hand it over to the payee after the payroll voucher was signed.

During the day, the pay table was never abandoned. Both the pay officer and the NCO would eat their lunch in the pay room. If the NCO went to the restroom, the pay officer would secure the pay room. If the pay officer went to the restroom, the NCO was in charge of security. Only the pay officer could disburse the pay; the only function of the NCO was to act as the pay officer's security guard. As was the usual custom, not all the soldiers were paid—due to leaves or personnel attending off post-military schools. In any case, the signed pay vouchers along with the unpaid vouchers with the cash not disbursed were taken back for final audit by the finance office. Now came the background music from *Jaws*, for the pay officer was holding his breath and hoping he was not "short" in his accounts. If the officer was short, he was on the hook and owed the money. It was the responsibility of the pay officer to balance his accounts; otherwise, Uncle Sam extended his arm, and as an officer and gentleman, he had to pay. Thank God I was never short!

A Payroll Officer, Not by the Book, September 1970

In September of 1970, the lucky pay officer in Charlie Company was Lieutenant "G," who was a rather personable young second lieutenant performing the duties of pay officer for the first time. A tall, athletic, and popular lieutenant, he received his commission through the ROTC program in college. He was recently married, had no children, and was considered a favorite in the battalion. On this particular day, Lieutenant G was doing all the duties I described above. Around 13:00 hours, Lieutenant G needed to go to the restroom; however, his NCO was out securing a late lunch for both him and the pay officer. Lieutenant M happened to be in the pay room when Lieutenant G asked Lieutenant M to guard the pay table with the cash and vouchers while he ran to the restroom. In true Army tradition, there is a code of honor between officers to protect and defend. Lieutenant M agreed, and Lieutenant G proceeded to the restroom. In this time lapse of a few minutes, Lieutenant M pocketed several thousand dollars from the pay table. When Lieutenant G returned to his duties, he continued his pay procedures and then repaired for his audit at the finance office. Do you hear the background music from *Jaws* again? This time the shark attacked, and Lieutenant G was indeed on the hook!

Immediately upon finding out about Lieutenant G's shortage, the CID (Criminal Investigation Division) was assigned to investigate. Within three days, Lieutenant M broke down and confessed to his transgression. Shame had come from this major transgression to the First Battalion, Seventh Infantry. Lieutenant M was a struggling young first lieutenant who was married with one child; he couldn't make ends meet; and he had no money. He was court-martialed and relieved of his duties.

The whole scenario smacked of the old TV program called *Branded*. The rest of Lieutenant M's life would be a reflection of what he did on this one day in September of 1970. I detested what he did, but deep down inside, I felt sorry for him and his young family. On the other hand, the handsome and handpicked Goody Two-Shoes of the battalion, Lieutenant G, was given the punishment of never having to have the responsibility of being pay officer again. Such a punishment and such torture never having to have that responsibility again.

The Conniving Captain, 1970–1971

After EIB training and testing was completed at Wildflecken, I was transferred to a mechanized line infantry company. I was introduced to my new CO, who had just arrived from a combat tour of Vietnam. He was Captain T, and he was a rare breed, for he was given a field commission for actions performed in combat in Vietnam. Captain T spent most of his career as an NCO who was drafted in 1954, serving in Korea and later serving two tours of Vietnam in which he served as a member of an A detachment in Ki Ki with the Special Forces. It happened that Captain T was with this remote detachment when their position was overrun on Thanksgiving Day of 1969.

He was given a battlefield commission for his exploits, but deep inside, something rang phony with Captain T. It just so happened that as I came into A Company, the rather older captain took a liking to me. His wife was at least five years younger than he was, and they'd had a baby in 1970. He invited me over to his quarters for dinner, which I appreciated as a break from my usual routine of going to the O-Club. It became a ritual for him to invite me for barbecues, and eventually good old Captain T invited me on his pursuit of local girl chasing in A'Burg. Yes, that's right—this stellar married captain of the line was out womanizing with the local fraüleins, and I was to be his accomplice. Not that I'm a choirboy, but I felt very uncomfortable as Captain T scored time and time again with the local German girls while ironically, I, as a single bachelor, couldn't score no matter how I tried. As I saw it, Captain T was out of control, and by the way, he was having trouble getting into to his uniforms due to gaining weight. Life in the zone suited him well—too much Wiener schnitzel and beer. His uniforms were harder to get into.

Captain T's exploits soon became known to all personnel in A Company. It got so bad that First Sergeant Schmidt had a hard time finding our leader. The good captain would often take off on his motorcycle with a local German girl. Top (the army nickname for first sergeant) had the unenviable task of covering for all of Captain T's indiscretions. Repeatedly, Top told white lies to battalion headquarters in his loyalty to his commanding officer. The same held true for all the lieutenants in A Company—mum was the word. In fact, it became a running joke from First Sergeant Schmidt that he would have to cut orders for the XO (executive officer) to be acting commander in Captain T's constant absences.

Later, after I became the senior first lieutenant and the XO of A Company, Top would joke that I should go into acting in the theater, for it seemed I was always the "acting" commander. Such was the burden that all A Company lieutenants and Top had to bear while under the command of the ever-fattening Captain T. As time passed by, I tried to keep my distance from Captain T; however, he was my boss, and I was required to work with him. In the back of my mind, I sensed that he was nothing more than a "lifer," utilizing all his charm and talents on chasing women and furthering his military career no matter what the cost … or who he hurt and stepped on along his career path.

First Sergeant Schmidt, A Company, First
Battalion, Seventh Infantry, 1970–1971

First Sergeant Schmidt was not German. Top was actually born Ukrainian. In 1944, his family was wiped out entirely, with the exception of his mother surviving, when the Russians attacked as part of the Operation Begration in the East against Germany in their ultimate march into Berlin. At the tender age of fourteen, Top and his mother were homeless and trekking westward toward Germany, seeking food and shelter. Once arriving in West Prussia, he was conscripted in the Hitler Youth Corps and actually ended up fighting his antagonists. Life in the buffer zone of the Ukraine and Belarus, which was known as the land of *lebensraum* of East Germany, had proved to be an area of intense fighting and destruction. Along with fighting side by side with the Nazis, Top took on the German surname of Schmidt. Such was Top's hatred of everything connected to the Soviet regime.

At the end of the war, Top and his mother were nothing but displaced persons in a war-torn Germany. In time, he and his mother shipped out to the United States and settled in Detroit, Michigan, where Top took on a position in a General Motors assembly plant. By the early 1950s, he was drafted into the US Army and subsequently went to basic training and Advance Infantry School; he then landed up with the Second Infantry Division in South Korea. He again had the privilege of hearing the sounds of guns. In fact, he was a member of a machine gun company that went up Pork Chop Hill in one of the last major engagements of the Korean War. As luck would have it, the private survived this traumatic experience. Hence Private Schmidt decided to make the army his home and career. He later married and started a family, which I never met. He was protective of his family, and I imagined that he ran his household very much as he ran A Company.

With Top, the orderly room was his domain. If any lieutenant needed any paperwork of any kind, he had to request it personally from Top. There were no questions, and God help you if you touched anything in the orderly room without first seeking the permission of Top. He stood six feet one and weighed a solid, muscular 210 pounds.

His accent was a definite Eastern European dialect, and his eyes were straightforward, honest, and sincere. He was a professional soldier, the likes of which I had never seen before.

I knew he had served in WWII for the Nazis. He was at Pork Chop Hill in Korea and was present in the charge up Hamburger Hill with the 101st Airborne in Vietnam. In my presence, I was involved with a true professional; John Wayne and Arnold Schwarzenegger are merely fictional wise guys pretending to be heroes. What was rather remarkable is that Schmidt liked me and, in essence, always protected me. As I look back over the spectrum of forty-one years, Schmidt was the older brother I never had. He protected me and defended me; he gave me counsel and imparted his wisdom. He was a true professional soldier and, above all, a humanitarian whom I will always respect and admire. As I write these words, I wonder if he is still with us.

Wolfgang Dieter Yellowhorse, Aschaffenburg, 1970–1971

In the culture of what was then called postwar Europe, with Americans being the primary defenders of world democracy during this period called the Cold War, a culture played out in many intertwining subplots. There was a plethora of senior NCOs who were attached to the European way of life. Many of these career soldiers were indeed true Americans but spent very little time in the United States. They were lifers who were married to Germans they had met on previous tours, and in many instances, they melded into the life of their spouses' families. These soldiers constantly sought to be stationed in Germany. Many were Vietnam and Korean War veterans, very much like First Sergeant Schmidt. They rarely lived in military housing, almost always living on the West German economy. As the navy and marine personnel were prone to be stationed in the Far East or in Southeast Asia, Japan, and the Philippines, many army personnel sought duty in Germany. In essence, this developed a culture all its own, which started with the US occupation of Europe.

At Graves Kaserne, we had several lifelong soldiers of West Germany; they lived with the Germans and even fluently spoke the German language. One officer who immediately caught my attention was our motor pool officer Lieutenant Wolfgang Dieter Yellowhorse. Lieutenant Yellowhorse was born in Germany to a German mother and a Native American sergeant who was stationed in Germany after World War II.

Wolfgang was an army brat who, at the young age of eighteen, joined the army and was sent to Vietnam for a one-year tour of duty as a door gunner on a Huey helicopter. He came back as a buck sergeant, went to OCS, and was duly commissioned a second lieutenant. He immediately did as Bob and I had done and signed voluntary indefinite in order to be assigned in West Germany. Lieutenant Yellowhorse had a BOQ room, and God knows why, as he was never there. Being able to speak fluent German, he was the hit of all the local fraüleins. If you wanted to go to a good restaurant, only say the word and Wolfgang would know where to go, what to order, and have the locals eating out of his hand. Life was good for Wolfgang Dieter Yellowhorse. Since I left the battalion in May 1971, I never again heard from that wild and crazy enigma of the American Indian who spoke fluent German.

First Sergeant Schmidt and First Lieutenant Geschke
December 1970

CHAPTER 11

WEST GERMANY: A WINTER'S TALE

A Company, First Battalion, Seventh Infantry was my home from August 1970 to May 1971. My new boss was Captain T, and the new first sergeant was Schmidt. A Company spent the first three months of my new assignment in garrison at Graves Kaserne. During this time span, I was assigned a mechanized infantry platoon of the line. Also given to me was the responsibility of the oversight of company M-16 rifle qualifications. This required expertise in the supervision of KD and pop-up targets' operational ranges.

I had the opportunity to interact with the Third Infantry Division Advanced Marksmanship Unit, which was logistically attached to our battalion. The personnel assigned to this unit were from all ranks, from private first class (PFC) to the field-grade rank of major. These men were world-class small arms weapons experts.

The weapons utilized by this unit ranged from the .45-caliber pistol to the operation of a .50-caliber machine gun. To give the reader an appreciation of who these "weapons experts" were, I'll categorize the groups and types of shooters. A small cadre of experts consisted of experienced combat "killer snipers" who'd each served at least one tour of duty as a sniper in Vietnam. Killer sniper teams were used in the clandestine Operation Phoenix. This operation was the ultimate covert top-secret operation that essentially targeted Vietcong leadership. The mission of these highly trained sniper groups was to destroy the leadership infrastructure of the Vietcong. Another group of this unit consisted of competitive shooters of excellent distinction who competed throughout the world, including Olympic competitions.

World-Class Marksmen

It was my privilege to observe and learn from true professionals. I was instructed in the finer nuances of range operations, including the utilization of my AIs (assistant instructors) for maximum control and efficiency. Included in this broad education in the use of small arms, I was instructed on how to handle weapon malfunctions in the line of fire.

During this time of gaining weapons proficiency, my company commander was continuing his chase of the local women, driving drove around A'Burg on his brand-new Honda 750 motorcycle. As time passed at Graves Kaserne, Top (First Sergeant Schmidt) was kept busy hiding the fact that the old man (Captain T the commanding officer) was hardly around to "command." Truth be told, it was Top who actually ran the company, but that's a secret between you and me. Ever-loyal Top was like Houdini performing magical illusions, convincing battalion headquarters that the old man was actually there and in full command. As Detective Foyle from the famous TV series *Mystery Theatre* would say, "Right!" Little did his superiors realize that this married combat veteran was acting like a rebellious teenager gone wild. His behavior was not conducive to being a true combat officer of a combat line unit.

In due time, the company was preparing to participate in the Third Infantry Division maneuvers in Granfenwoehr, which would take place over a two-week span. As our vehicles left by railhead, I held my breath as I became the senior lieutenant, thus promoting me to XO of A Company.

Granfenwoehr, November 1970

By the calendar, winter always begins on December 21. However, in the land where the ghosts of Hitler's panzers still roam, the weather takes on the early signs of a nasty winter in this, the eleventh month.

Not that Graf was like Siberia; however, it harbored the kind of cold that sends shivers down one's spine. As we secured our equipment on the first day, we were preparing for an extended stay on the fields of Graf. I had been comfortable with my duties as a platoon leader; however, the responsibilities of XO and being second in command were strange and unwelcome.

My Introduction to "Infantry Weather"

As we headed out, all I remember was a gray and overcast sky with the temperatures in the mid-thirties. The fields were thoroughly muddy, and as we headed out, sleet like rain was pelting my face. Traveling at thirty miles per hour over rough terrain with pellets hitting you straight on, one could almost wish for the jungle heat of Southeast Asia. In other words, Graf was no picnic, as any GI who experienced it would testify. My take on this scene made me utter these words as far as the fields of Graf: "My God, this is infantry weather." To this day, when I experience severe conditions, I'll mutter aloud, "I see we're experiencing infantry weather." In all reality, this lifetime experience emanated from that piece of real estate still controlled by the US Army in Grafenwoehr. The terrain, the weather, the mud, the fog, the cold, and the smells still haunt my soul. Such was the life of an infantryman while operating in the fields of Graf.

Moving out! Granfenwoehr, November 1970

77

Maneuvers in the Soup!

As a rather junior officer of the line, I had no idea what was to happen in the next several days out in the muddy tundra that was Graf. Our movements were speedy and precise. We moved forward in short bursts, and in true zone form, our turrets revolved in reverse, and our track drivers took on their familiar role in heading west with guns pointed east. My son, who is an artist, should paint this picture so indelibly imbedded in my memory. The strategy of our army was that we were but a delaying force and were mere fodder in the initial attrition of what was to be Armageddon.

As night settled in at the rather early hour of 16:30 hours, we set up our defensive position. The weather at this hour showed an intense fog rolling in a soup-like atmosphere in the twilight. By 18:00 hours, it was completely dark, and the "soup" limited visibility to approximately ten yards. In support of our mechanized APCs, we had elements from the Fourth of the Sixty-Fourth Armor Battalion with us as we circled into an NDP (night defensive position). Captain T was stellar in all the fast maneuvers that transpired during the day, as his land navigation was impeccable.

As good as the old man was in his navigation sightings, he constantly double-checked his positions with Top. First Sergeant Schmidt was ever more precise. As I monitored and mentally noted all the movements, I recognized the main elements of topographical sightings, but as good as I thought I was, Captain T was better, and Top was better than a modern-day GPS. He could pinpoint a location within ten meters. I was good with a map and compass, but these guys brought land navigation to a new level.

Today our troops utilize computers and GPS systems to know where they are. The art and science of topographical land navigation utilizing a topographical map with a compass and the ability to convert a one-dimensional map to a three-dimensional vision or sighting is fast becoming a lost skill. As we get older, we say that they don't make them like they used to. In our day, we utilized our wits and senses, and you know what? We were pretty damned good at it!

As dark turned to a pitch-black night, Captain T gave me an

assignment that I shall call the turning point in my military career. It was approximately 21:00 hours when the old man gave me the grid coordinates for battalion headquarters and ordered me to proceed to that position along with my jeep driver, enemy prisoner, and a coded message. As I exited the APC, I actually stumbled onto the muddy field trying to locate my jeep. I could hardly see anything.

Once in the vehicle, we could only put on the blackout lights— this was so the enemy couldn't see us. The problem was that I had to let my eyes adjust, for the "soup" was getting thicker. Quite literally, we traveled at about five miles per hour, and every twenty-five meters or so, I had to exit the jeep and shoot an azimuth with my compass, walk back to the jeep, and proceed onward. I used known terrain features sifting through the thick fog in this slow and agonizing process. Dark as hell in the mud and literally in the "soup," the only thing I heard was the pounding of my anxious heart. How the hell did I get into this mess!

I finally arrived at my destination. I knew I hit the mark perfectly, but there was no battalion headquarters. I saw numerous mud tracks from tracked and wheeled vehicles, along with a myriad of footprints. Headquarters had been there—and just recently, like within the last hour or so—but it wasn't there when I arrived. Headquarters had moved out, lock, stock, and barrel. I was out in the middle of nowhere—with my jeep, driver, the "prisoner," and the coded message.

Oh No!

Hurrying to my jeep-mounted radio to transmit my findings, I did the clumsiest thing of my life. Remember Ralphie in the classic movie *A Christmas Story*, when he shoots his BB gun and hits his glasses, breaking them? His reaction was the inevitable "Oh no!" Well, picture a rather junior XO accidentally sitting on the radio microphone and breaking it. *Oh no!* I'd just cut off all communication back to the old man. No communication, along with the wrong coordinates given by my boss. I had no choice but to return to the company NDP. Unlike Ralphie, I had no story to concoct. I remember my father dressing me down and making me feel bad for doing the wrong thing. Captain T not only dressed me down, but he embarrassed me with his rant of expletives, which I'm sure are still hovering above Graf to this day. He was trying to lead me to believe that I failed in the mission. I, on the other hand, knew that something was not right!

The Caper Is Revealed

The next morning, Top came to me and guided me to an isolated field area, where he told me that I was not to blame for the battalion headquarters fiasco. He told me that headquarters had moved two hours prior to my leaving the NDP, and that Captain T was informed of that movement and given the new coded coordinates. Top knew that the old man never decoded the coordinates, nor did he write the new coordinates down. What he ordered me to do was with the "old" coordinates, meaning that battalion headquarters had moved to another location. His orders to me were incorrect. As good a combat officer as Captain T was, he lacked attention to detail in that instance. I looked at Top incredulously and said, "I knew I hit my marker!"

When I confronted the old man, all he could do was admonish me again! All I did was take note of this incident of treachery of an officer who had tremendous battlefield skills but possessed no honor and was willing to lie about *his* mistake at the expense of a junior officer. His motives were nothing more than political, and I resented his actions. To this day, if I met him, I would tell him straight up of the treachery of his actions. At that moment, it became clear to me that not all officers have honor or are gentlemen, as in life there are people who only think of themselves. My only mistake was to sit on a transmitting microphone that was severed from the radio. I'll never do that again!

Vilseck, January 1971

Thanksgiving passed and the routine of Graves Kaserne continued in its usual routine in December 1970. By midmonth, we had a picturesque Bavarian snowfall much like the winters on the borders of Lake Erie in the lands of the Western Reserve of Northeast Ohio. The routine continued to Christmas, when lo and behold, I drew the lucky straw to be officer of the day on Christmas Day. Supposedly, the duty roster of the officer of the day is maintained by the S-1 (personnel office); somehow this duty was manipulated, for I was not even close to being the next officer in line—politics and chicanery became the political rule. I knew that Captain T had me on his shit list. As a subordinate officer, I was at the mercy of Captain T. During this time span, Top knew of my dilemma and kept telling me to report these actions to battalion brass. I marked the time and continued with my duties.

In January 1971, we received orders as a company to disembark by rail to Vilseck, Germany, which was a US Army Training School on the real estate of the grand Grafenwoehr expanse. We arrived by railhead with all our track vehicles, only there was one key person missing at the railhead in Vilseck. That's right. Captain T was not there. He was gallivanting about the Bavarian countryside with a fraülein with whom he would spend four days. Top was at a loss as to what to do. Here we were in Vilseck, without our vaunted leader. As I sat in our compound orderly room, Top said, "Sir, I believe you should have taken thespian lessons while attending college."

I responded, "What in the hell are you talking about, Sarge?"

"Well, sir, I have to cut orders for you to be acting commanding officer without the presence of Captain T." It still amazes me that the bastard never got dressed down!

It is true that our two-week duty was a piece of cake. All the line officers had to do was lead our platoons to the training areas at 07:00 hours and turn over command to the training officers. It was a tough job, but someone had to do it! By 17:00 hours, all officers would retire to the Vilseck O-Club for drinks and dinner. Life was good!

On the fifth day, Captain T came strolling into the O-Club for drinks and dinner. Keep in mind that we hadn't seen our "leader" for the past four days. As he strode into our huddle of officers imbibing our first drinks, he stated emphatically for all to hear, "You guys really have it made. This is the life!"

I looked him straight in the eye and said, "Well, sir, at least we're here!"

As God is my witness, he turned to me and said, "You'll regret you ever said that!"

I can actually say that what I said was not only right, but I'll say to this day that my convictions represent the basis of truth, which is seldom present in the political realm. The old man was so embarrassed that he stormed out of the room.

Lieutenant Mike Bishop, whose father was on active duty as a full colonel, looked to all the rather stunned officers in attendance and said, "Whoa, Geschke, I can't believe you had the balls to say what each of us should have also said!"

To Captain T, I say:

> *I am no sheep; I am no dog*
> *Nor Councillor, and no shellfish—.*
> *I have remained a wolf, my heart*
> *And all my fangs are wolfish.*
> *Heinrich Heine, Germany.*
> *A Winter's Tale*
> *Hamburg, September 17, 1844*

The frozen tundra of Vilseck, January 1971

CHAPTER 12

IN BERLIN: THE MAGIC
NUMBER WAS THREE

*There is one sign the Soviets can make that would be
unmistakable, that would advance dramatically the cause of
freedom and peace. General Secretary Gorbachev, if you seek
peace, if you seek prosperity for the Soviet Union and Eastern
Europe, if you seek liberalization, come here to this gate. Mr.
Gorbachev, open this gate. Mr. Gorbachev, tear down this wall!*

Ronald Reagan, June 12, 1987
West Berlin, Germany
In front of the Brandenburg Gate
Commemorating the 750th anniversary of Berlin

After the Jordan alert and my initial encounter in Grafenwoehr,
I was seeking a three-day pass out of the constraints of
A'Burg. Life in the zone was starting to grind on my good
humor. What to do? Alas, the lightbulb went on, and I called bouncing
Bobo (Couch's nickname for Bob) in Berlin. Now, mind you, the
telecommunications in West Germany on the American military
lines resembled telephone operations of the States relative to the
1930s. When I dialed Bob in Berlin, a recording would say, "Berlin.
Dial your number." I would rotary dial the appropriate number, and
bouncing Bobo would answer.

As it transpired, I told Bob that I had a three-day pass to travel
at my leisure and asked if I could see him in Berlin. Toto, being

accommodating, said he'd secure the necessary "flag orders" for the duty train from Frankfurt to West Berlin. Within that very week, I received the flag orders, with the stars and stripes and all the proper signatures and credentials. All I had to do was follow the yellow brick road, and unlike Dorothy, who traveled with Toto, my objective was to arrive in the outpost city to meet Toto.

Flag Orders and the Duty Train

The duty train from Frankfurt to Berlin left the bahnhof at 20:00 hours. The reason for the late night departure was due to the insistence of the East German government—so that we passengers could not see the drab run-down conditions of their infrastructure under the shroud of darkness. Another quirk of the Cold War, playing little games and thinking we were too dumb to notice! In June, however, the nights in the northern hemisphere of Germany remained light way late into the night. Also, morning came early, and eighteen-hour days were the norm in the third week of June. Hence, if one stayed awake, one got a bird's-eye view of what living in communist East Germany would be like.

As we made our run to Berlin, our obsession with the number three began. It would take three different locomotives to finish our trek to the outpost city. The first engine would take us from Frankfurt to the rail checkpoint of the East German frontier, where we would switch locomotives. East Germans conducted and engineered the new locomotive on our trip through East Germany. At the border of West Berlin, we would hit another checkpoint, where another locomotive was coupled to our train, and we would proceed to the West Berlin bahnhof. Since my curiosity got the best of me, I hardly slept, and I was able to observe the drabness and dark feeling of seeing life in the mist and cover of a June night in Nordic Germany. We would arrive in West Berlin almost twelve hours from the time we left. It was approximately 07:30 hours when Toto greeted me at the end of that yellow brick road.

The troop train represented one of three ways to enter West Berlin. The other two ways were by air flight and travel by vehicle, utilizing one of three autobahns available for travel in 1970. Again, the number three rings significantly in the mentioning of the outpost city.

A Toto Moment

After the wall was erected, the duty trains continued to pass the various checkpoints and change locomotives—but with one big difference. Russian soldiers with loaded weapons boarded the train and searched each compartment. Imagine the terror of the passengers. Sometime during the early 1960s, the state departments of the UK, France, and the United States came up with the system of "flag orders."

The train commander had to verify each passenger with an ID card and flag orders showing the nationality of the passenger, thus stopping the boarding scenario. While waiting for the locomotive change at Checkpoint Bravo, we waited until the soldiers were close to the toilet car and then flushed the toilets, attempting to spray the soldiers and their German shepherd police dogs. This literally "pissed" them off.

Checkpoint Charlie and East Berlin

Bob already had an itinerary in mind, which included crossing into East Berlin through the famed Checkpoint Charlie. This was planned for the afternoon; in the meantime, we drove in Bob's trusty VW Beetle to his BOQ. Up to this point, I haven't described my BOQ in A'Burg, mainly because of its rather unremarkable decor, which could best be described as "early college dorm," with fifteen-year-old furniture that showed its wear. In complete contrast to my living quarters, Lieutenant Toto had a master suite complete with modern furnishings, china, and silverware. Life for a bachelor officer of the Berlin Brigade came right out of *Better Homes & Gardens*. Good old bouncing Bobo, a staff officer living the high life in the outpost city, was making an officer of the line in the zone drool in envy. Fifteen months down the road, Toto would see what it was like to be an officer of the line.

As previously mentioned, we got into Bob's VW, and off we went in full Class A uniforms (dress greens) toward Checkpoint Charlie. Even though East Germany was technically our Cold War adversary, in keeping with the Potsdam Agreement, we were entering the "Russian Zone of Berlin," and in political reality, we were still considered postwar allies. Go figure!

The only requirement for entry was that we had to be in uniform. When we entered the checkpoint, our car was thoroughly inspected by the German authorities, which included the use of mirrors on the underside of the car to search for contraband or even people on the way out of East Berlin. As I stated before, during the Cold War period, Berlin was the basis of many espionage novels and movies. When entering through the threshold of Checkpoint Charlie, we left the modern auspices of West Berlin in all its economic revelry and entered into the darkness of what remains of an East Berlin that is somewhat still showing the effects from the last battle for Berlin in 1945. In effect it was like going from the modern times of the '70s into the realm of what Berlin was just after World War II. I saw standing and operational buildings with shrapnel markings pocking the outside appearance of buildings. Bob and I saw young children running to us, begging for treats of candy and such. If I didn't know any better, I would think I was living the GI's life of my father during WWII.

Flag Shops and Spooks

As Bob took me to what the GIs of West Berlin called the "flag shops" of East Berlin, I noticed that German polizei were following us in a dark and rather drab Eastern European automobile; they were monitoring our every move. As this was happening, I thought, *Now I'm the one playing out the dramatics that were prevalent on the American movie screens, about the exotic spy versus spy drama of the Cold War era.*

As it was, Bob and I were entering nothing more than a political communistic propaganda store that sold all the popular accoutrements known to all as the standard of known communist genre seen worldwide. The articles included North Vietnamese flags, North Korean flags, East German flags, and the hammer and sickle of the Soviet flag. Along with the flags, there was an array of posters, current political busts, and newly minted communist coins. Everything of the Eastern European Communist ilk ran rampant in this political shop. They also had beautiful handcrafted ship models, and I bought one. I still have it in my library today. As I perused the shop, I came across a bust that was a remarkable likeness of Nikita Khrushchev. I mentioned this likeness to Bob, and the storekeeper came rushing to my side, exclaiming, *"Nein, nein!"* Obviously, the name of Khrushchev was no long in favor in the world of Communist East Berlin. Silly me!

I could just hear it being played out: the East Berlin polizei barging into the shop and taking Bob and me down to the interrogation room. I had visions of these actions being blown out of proportion, making it cause for an international incident. So much for my daydream. What really happened was that Bob and I both apologized, proceeded to make our purchases, and went on our merry way. Again, the East Berlin polizei followed our every turn as we proceeded back to the safe haven of Checkpoint Charlie and the light and freedom of West Berlin.

Spandau

Toto took me to all the normal West Berlin attractions, which included a ride down the Ku'damm, seeing the bombed-out Kaiser-Wilhelm Gedachtniskirche Cathedral of West Berlin, and a trip to the British sector to see the infamous Spandau Prison (at that time, it had only one prisoner: Rudolph Hess). Life in West Berlin was exciting, and you could see that the Berliners appreciated the American GI. Unlike the West Germans in the zone, the West Berliners were always mindful of what our mission and purpose were. They never forgot the Berlin Airlift. In fact, there is a famous sculpture representing the three air corridors used by the American Air Force during the "airlift" of food and supplies so ordered by President Truman in 1948. Truman showed Stalin and the people of Berlin that the United States was standing steadfast in this showdown in the outpost city. The Berliners always remembered that, and it stayed with them until the wall came down in 1989.

My first visit to West Berlin ended, and Bob drove me to the West Berlin bahnof. As the troop train headed due west toward Frankfurt that Sunday night, I again spied on the dusky drabness that was East Germany. I didn't know it then, but I realized later that the lives of the people living under the veil of communism were acting on the promises of an ultimate lie. What was explained to them was not true and could never happen. They were living under the auspices of a misguided philosophy which could and would never happen. These people were never told the truth, and their hopes and dreams would never come to fruition using the communist form of governance. It wouldn't happen until the old ways of communism became economically unfeasible and the lie could not sustain itself any longer. However, I was young and dumb as I headed back to the zone, where we, as soldiers of the Cold War, would show our false bravado and laugh in the face of that Russian bear.

Berlin, March 1971

"Berlin. Dial your number." I dialed the Berlin number and Bob Toto answered the phone. I immediately told him that I'd be coming to Berlin that weekend with the First of the Seventh basketball team. My job, which I eagerly volunteered for, was essentially to babysit the enlisted personnel. My job requirements included making sure the team members were where they were supposed to be at all appointed times. I made sure the troops were quartered and fed, and I attended two games during the weekend. On Saturday evening, I had free time, and Bob and I headed to the Berlin O-Club, later going back to his quarters for more libations. During this trip, I didn't have time to see the sights, but I did get to meet many of Bob's peers who worked and lived with him in the outpost city.

Taking in the Sights of Berlin as a Babysitter

The social life in Berlin was much more diverse and interesting than back in the zone. We stayed up until two in the morning, which was something that rarely happened, even on a Saturday evening back in A'Burg. The next day, we had breakfast with the team and went on to the arena, where the team won the championship game.

Once the team showered and dressed, I had to account for all personnel and make sure that each of them had their flag orders. Most of the players were African Americans, and this was their first time out in the big city of Germany. They were excited about winning and excited to be where they were. It was my job as their officer to temper their enthusiasm. As we boarded the train, I made sure all personnel were accounted for and in their proper seats. The train left the West Berlin bahnof on time at 20:00 hours, and shortly thereafter, we had our first locomotive switch on the East German border.

And that's when the fun began. The train had to stop for the switch, of course. No problem, right? Oh, no! My EM (enlisted men) see Russian soldiers pacing the sides of the duty train, inspecting for escaped personnel or contraband. My men opened their coach windows and shouted obscenities at the Soviets. Oh, great, here we go again—another international incident of the East German border. I immediately rushed to the area where the ruckus emanated from, ordering an immediate halt to their antics. I was mad, and they knew it. I didn't reason with them; I gave them a direct order to shut up or I would order an Article 15. An Article 15 was misconduct charges enacted on a soldier; in the eyes of the army command, it was akin to getting a court-martial. They shut up instantly. With this crisis avoided, all I could think of was getting back to Frankfurt without incident—and back to A'Burg. For once, A'Burg didn't look so bad at all.

Berlin, June 1971
Drab and Bleak

"Berlin. Dial your number." I dialed Bob and told him I again wanted to partake in the unusual sights and sounds of the outpost city. Bob again provided the necessary flag orders, and off I went in the duty train as it trekked into the Nordic night so bright. I remember that as we approached West Berlin in the morning light, I saw East German workers walking the drab and shrapnel-pocked streets to their jobs.

All I could think was, *God, what an existence they must live. What do they have to look forward to?* The premise of their work, their lives, and their political system was based on lies and half-truths, with the carrot being dangled in front of them, suggesting that things would surely get better.

This is what I saw in 1971, from my perspective as a citizen soldier serving my country in this faraway land. By "faraway," I'm not just stating that we were thousands of miles from home. I am speaking of our lives lived in a democracy with freedom of expression and of economic diversity, where one can strive to live the life one wants to live. So as the train pulled into the West Berlin bahnof, I was feeling somewhat lucky to be an American and somewhat sympathetic to the people who lived a far different life behind the Iron Curtain. At the time I was living this life in Germany, no one could even imagine that this status quo would ever change, at least in my lifetime. One could only think that this standoff, which was punctuated by the very existence of Berlin, would continue forever. It would take eighteen years to prove me wrong, when the people living behind the Iron Curtain would see that it was indeed a big lie and that the perpetrators could no longer convince the populace that all would be well.

I Become a Target

As always, bouncing Bobo was there to greet me at the bahnof. This time the itinerary was based on the tour of the wall from all angles short and tall, grand and grotesque in all its pre-graffiti glory. This was the grand tour of the wall prior to the time of West Germans writing their expressions for all to see on the iron curtain of injustice. I remember Bob taking me to the bridge that goes nowhere. Quite literally, this bridge crossed a waterway; the only thing was that in the middle of the bridge were rolls of concertina wire, preventing anyone from crossing into East Berlin and preventing East Berliners from crossing into West Berlin. Toto yelled at me when I got too close to the wire: "Christ, Geschke, the guard in that tower has a bead on you; get the hell out of there!" I remember looking up, and sure enough, the rifle was following my every move as I waved the peace sign and gradually backed off, returning to the soil of West Berlin. Here it is, forty years later, and Toto reminded me that the East German guard had an SKS rifle that was more accurate at long ranges rather than the conventional AK-47.

The Gateway to Prussia

It seems as if I were preordained to maintaining excitement levels each and every time I came to visit the outpost city. We gratefully left the bridge to nowhere and went on to see the Russian Memorial, which was quite near the Brandenburg Gate. Both the Russian Memorial and the Brandenburg Gate were located in East Berlin; however, we were able to take a picture of the memorial from Bob's moving VW and shoot several pictures of the Brandenburg Gate from an elevated platform over the wall, which was located in West Berlin, of course.

Back to Spandau Prison

We also traveled to Spandau Prison, which was located in the British sector. As mentioned, there was only one prisoner left from the Nuremberg Trials, and that was Rudolph Hess, who was Hitler's next in command until he inexplicitly flew himself to Great Britain to negotiate a settlement with that country. Hess would remain at Spandau until he died in 1987.

Immediately after his death, the prison was razed, and all remnants of that prison were destroyed. The intent of this action was to make sure that nothing would be left of any signs of Nazism forever. The intention of this action was not to encourage a new Nazi movement. As a point of interest, this prison was operated by all the four powers—the United States, Great Britain, France, and Russia—as part of the Potsdam Agreement. This operation stayed in effect until 1987, just two years prior to the demise of communism in East Europe. The rotation of the operation and responsibilities of prisoner care were ceremonially changed at a "change of command ceremony," which rotated on a monthly basis. It must be remembered that it was at the insistence of the USSR that these procedures stayed in effect until the last prisoner died. In the long memories of the Russian bear, they would never forgive any German who caused them pain in the "Great Patriotic War." Such was the mentality and demeanor of these Cold War warriors as they settled into their strategies and tactics of a long, hard winter.

The Ancient City by the Marshes

Bob and I spent the rest of Saturday downing our libations and catching up on what was transpiring in our respective current assignments. We spent the next day touring more spots of the wall, and soon it was time to go. This would be my third and final visit to Berlin. As the years have gone by, I've watched some travel shows of Berlin. God knows I looked at the current modern buildings on which some of the most famous architects, such as Frank Gehry, have done their work and wondered if Berlin had any resemblance to what I remembered from back in 1970 and 1971.

Berlin, a vibrant and eclectic metropolis, has reinvented itself many times. The city was founded in the twelfth century on the embankment of marshes, and it has survived the Middle Ages, Bismarck, WWI, and the scourge of Hitler. It has evolved. The last major challenge of this city was the Cold War, in which Berlin was the focal point and represented the strife and legacy of a conflict of ideology. The Cold War began with the Berlin Airlift during the Truman administration and ended with the symbolic tearing down of the wall during the Bush administration. In between, the speech given by President Kennedy at the face of the Brandenburg Gate and Reagan's "Tear down this wall!" speech right in front of the gates conveyed the thoughts of all free men everywhere.

Berlin was the symbol of the Cold War. It represented the nerve center of an epic struggle that many of us today seem to have long forgotten. I wonder if the current Berliners have any concept of what transpired in the Nordic German city. My hope is that what we as Allies, and specifically the United States will be remembered in its endeavors during the "long, hard winter' of the Cold War. May it be so, that we will never be forgotten, and that history will duly record these unselfish and meaningful actions done by a victor of war to the aid of a defeated enemy. In looking back at what major powers have done to their vanquished foes, I can think of no other major country aiding their defeated foes as the United States did at the end of World War II.

During the Cold War, the essence of the Berlin Brigade in the outpost city was a symbolic gesture showing communism that democracy was a viable option. The military presence was symbolic, while knowing in reality that this military unit stood no chance of surviving an actual attack. Thus the personnel assigned to this elite unit were indeed handpicked. We in the zone were true field soldiers who had to endure a soldier's life, while the Berlin Brigade was the shining star exhibited as the "proud peacock," showing our adversaries that we never had to lie about who we were and how we accomplished the deeds we did. Long live the outpost city.

Geschke and Toto
The Bridge to Nowhere, Berlin Summer 1971

Toto and Geschke
The Brandenburg Gate, Berlin Summer 1971

Berlin Airlift Monument, in front of Tempelhof Airport, 1970

Bombed out WWII East Berlin building, 1970

Chapter 13
In Transition

My father always said
Never be comfortable in your position.
For life is full of surprises,
And living it proper
Is nothing but one lifelong transition.
Times may be troubled but
Stay the course;
That too will change.
Times may be good but
Stay the course;
As that also will change.
Take nothing for granted;
Live life to the fullest each and every day.
Extra effort and due diligence
Will pay you back many fold.
Self-pity and complaining
Are the tools of a loser.
When in transition,
Think good thoughts.
For if one wallows in the bad thoughts
Of injustice and unfairness,
One may transition onto failure.
When things change,
Think positive and life will reward you!
                    —Richard C. Geschke, summer of 1971

A s we headed back to A'Burg following our field time in Vilseck, I knew my days in a line unit were numbered. I had gained the respect of my fellow junior officers after the Captain T incident. In fact, word got around to the rest of the battalion of what had happened, and several officers of the line, including some captains and other lieutenants who had previously ignored me, came to me with words of admiration and respect. Well, this being all well and good along with First Sergeant Schmidt, who always supported me, I still had to deal with the fact that Captain T was still my boss, and that I had to work for him in garrison as well as the field.

The Winds of Change

Once we settled into the routine of garrison duty at the kaserne, I began to notice that our company strength was shrinking every week; our company manpower was being reduced at an alarming rate. We still had the full complement of officers and senior NCOs; however, the EM of the ranks of E5 and below were disappearing due to enlisted terminations and recurrent rotations to Vietnam. This phenomena of lost manpower was not indigenous to A Company but was fast becoming the problem of filling the ranks of TO&E (Table of Organization and Equipment) throughout USAREUR (US Army Europe Command) in the early part of 1971.

Southeast Asia Making Its Mark in Germany

Vietnam was taking its toll on all operations in the zone of Germany. Not only were we losing personnel, but our equipment was aging and not being replaced with new equipment. The more advanced and new equipment was earmarked by first priority to Vietnam, even though we were then beginning to pull our combat units out of Southeast Asia in the process called Vietnamization. The concept of Vietnamization was to gradually exit our combat units out of Vietnam and transition the ARVN (Army of the Republic of Vietnam) into the combat areas to fight the Vietcong and NVA (North Vietnam Army). I later found out as a staff officer in Da Nang that 90 percent of all the brand-new modern equipment was going straight to the ARVN.

Knowing that our training was to be rather limited, there was a process of mothballing up to half of all our equipment, which we did over a period of one month, and our battalion dwindled down to the strength of a reinforced company. The officers and NCOs could not conduct normal training in such areas of Grafenwohr or Wildflicken. With my situation with Captain T, life became downright uncomfortable, and I was looking for an inter-theater transfer. In other words, Get me the hell out of here. I went to the battalion S-1 (personnel office) and formally requested a transfer.

It should be noted that this was now March of 1971, and I had been in country for one year. Under our terms stated in the "vol-indef" agreement, we of that status were only guaranteed one year in our duty station of choice. Toto and I were beginning to hold our breath. However, both of us had our ears fixed to the rail and noticed that IOBC classes before us, such as IOBC 8-70, were not levied en masse as the other vol-indef classes had been before them. We also noticed that IOBC 7-70 waited fourteen months before being levied. With the Nixon Vietnamization program going full tilt, we started to hope that our military commitment would be thirty-six months and out in November of 1972, with no tour in Vietnam. Little did we know that these were just pipe dreams.

A Cripple in the Sky

I continued my duties in A'Burg into March of 1971, and we did most of our training out in the fields of Aschaffenburg. We were out with some APCs, along with my jeep, and we were testing our equipment when I heard a break in the squelch of the radio. I heard a frantic call coming over my frequency, which was our company's designated frequency. It was a pilot in a UH helicopter, frantically asking for directions for the helipad to division headquarters in Wurzburg. This guy was truly desperate as he conveyed that he was carrying a general officer and had lost his bearings. He was asking for guidance in landing his bird at Leighton Barracks in Wurzburg. As I heard his plea for help, I immediately got on the horn and asked, "What is your current direction? Please give me any known points that you see below. Over." At that point, I was completely surprised that a pilot who was responsible for a general officer of high rank would be lost.

The primary duties of a pilot are to have the technical ability to fly an aircraft and to be an expert in navigation while flying. The easiest navigation bar none is navigating in the air. The definition of a map is succinct and simple—it is a portion of the earth's surface as seen from above. So navigation as "seen from above" should be a no-brainer to an experienced pilot. If the officer was carrying a general, it would stand to reason that the pilot should be of field-grade rank, which is major or above. I was quite literally scratching my head on that one. Nevertheless, my questions were quickly answered.

"My current heading is north, and I'm following a rather large river, which I do believe is the Main River. Over."

My answer was short and direct: "Where was your starting point? Over."

His prompt response: "My starting point was Frankfurt. Over."

I immediately answered, "You're headed in the wrong direction. Turn a hundred and eighty degrees and head due south. You will pass Frankfurt and eventually be parallel to the autobahn. Follow the river until you see a castle on the Main next to a bridge due south and you will see the helipad of the Third Infantry Division, with the blue-and-white diagonal stripes of the division colors. That's your destination. Please verify landing. Over."

The pilot answered, "Wilco, will verify! I owe you one. What the hell's your name. Over."

"First Lieutenant Geschke. Over."

Twenty-five minutes later, the squelch was broken again. "Verifying landing at Leighton Barracks. You must be infantry. Over."

"Yes, sir, I wear the crossed rifles. Out." That was the last time I was out in the fields in the zone.

Reassignment in the Zone

March turned into April, and then it was May when I suddenly got a call from Battalion S-1 to report immediately. Not knowing what was up, I immediately went to the S-1 shop to find out. First

Lieutenant Mirakian told me that there was an opening up at Division Headquarters Company for a motor pool officer. Here was my chance to get out of the line and get away from Captain T. I knew nothing about the inner workings of a motor pool, but beggars can't be choosers—anything to get out of my current situation suited me just fine. I was told to report to the commander of headquarters company at Wurzburg, located at Leighton Barracks, for an interview.

Two days later, I found myself entering the rather swank office of Captain Uptight, an ADA (Air Defense Artillery) officer who had served one tour of duty in Vietnam. The interview went well, although I did detect a rather braggart nature of his prior military duty and learned that he had no use for infantry officers since in his mind they were vastly inferior to the other arms of the army. Though as an exception to me, he said that I seemed to have the inherent qualities of a "quality officer," whatever that meant. I should have known better, but it was because of my sheer desperation to get out of my situation with Captain T that I took his line and the transfer was made. Oh well, I was still young and foolish!

Within the week, I was told to report to my new job in Wurzburg. It was mid-May when I moved into my new quarters in Wurzburg, which was an upgrade from my surroundings in A'Burg. I reported to my commanding officer and was immediately introduced to his company orderly, who was a spec 5 (specialist fifth class, E-5), and who I instantly saw as the chief suck-ass, captain's little informant. It was as clear as the nose on my face that this person was nothing but the eyes and ears of an insecure officer who ran his company as if it were his own fiefdom. To make things worse, Division Headquarters loved the STRAC well-uniformed captain who fit the bill as the poster boy for what an officer should look like.

I found out that this company commander was no better than Captain T. He definitely had his own agenda, and he really didn't care whose feet he trampled on. I was still in his good graces, but in my mind, it was an accident waiting to happen. I was in no mood to put up with any political chicanery, and it didn't take long for the "shootout at the OK Corral," for at that point in my military career, I was going to tell it like it was. Enough of those small-minded sycophants who thought they commanded the legions of Napoleon!

Making Waves—I just can't help myself!

Within two weeks, at the end of May of 1971, we went on Division Headquarters' maneuvers, which essentially meant that we were to live in tents for a period of three days. So what—this wasn't like line units doing maneuvers out in the fields to me. We set up shop the first day and basically did a mill-around-mill exercise which in the army was an exercise in doing nothing where we transported field-grade officers around to their headquarters destinations. After chow in the field, we settled into our tents for the evening. All I wanted to do was catch some shut-eye.

Much to my chagrin, in came Captain Uptight, who proceeded to tell his tales of being a Vietnam veteran and how he single-handedly put the Vietcong in their place during his one-year tour of Vietnam. All night long, I heard one story after another about how his unit saved the infantry from the worst fate known to mankind. Instead of complimenting the good captain on his valor and military acumen, I simply stated to him, looking him straight in the eye, "It's late. I wish you would take your war stories to another tent! Good-night!"

Looking back, I guess I was talking out of turn. But it's what I felt, and I found out long ago that if one spends time talking about his combat exploits repeatedly, it's probably wishful thinking that never really occurred. It has taken me almost forty years to recollect what I've experienced, and it is very difficult to write about oneself in an objective way. I was again in the soup and now I had another "boss" who was angry with me.

Meeting the Mousy Captain!

Within the week, I was told to report to the assistant G-1 (division personnel) at Division Headquarters. I reported to this AG (Adjutant General's Corps) captain with thick glasses and a pronounced stutter. He was apologetic when informing me that Captain Uptight considered my appointment to division motor pool officer to be a mistake due to irreconcilable personality differences. As he continued to stutter out the standard lines of rejection, I told him that I felt Captain Uptight was a "prick of the first caliber," and now I was ready for him to give me my new assignment. In the back of my mind, I was laughing. The gung ho Vietnam vet hadn't had the balls to fire me himself. And I'd had enough of the political chicanery that those career-minded "masters of their own domain" weaved into the parlance of military protocol.

As my mind wandered and inside I was amused, the rather nerdy AG captain looked relieved and told me to report to Captain Feelgood at Division Special Services for my new assignment. I got up, saluted the good captain, and shook his hand. Finally, I had a REMF (rear echelon motherfucker) job. In my mind, I had sixteen months of doing a job in Germany and then back to civilian life. Little did I know! At that moment, I was mad, feeling that the military was nothing but a political battlefield played by small-minded people who took advantage of their subordinates. If the subordinates did not "play ball," the ball was taken away, no matter how good or competent they were. In the end, justice would be there, but during that time and place, I was wandering in limbo.

First Lieutenant Geschke
Leighton Barracks, Wurzburg 1971

Going to Heidelberg

Before I introduce you to Captain Feelgood, I must digress with a

Toto Moment written by me. Bob's parents were taking a European vacation, visiting Germany, Italy, and other countries on their extended holiday. Bob had called me earlier in the week and asked where we should take his parents out in the zone. I immediately thought of the lighting of the ancient castle in Heidelberg. This was a popular event observed several times a year, and the Bavarians considered it a fine local tradition rather than a local tourist trap. I picked up the Totos at the Frankfurt bahnof, and off we traveled on the autobahn, where Alfred Toto was appalled at my speeding. Bob, who was in the back with his mother, tried to explain to his shotgun-riding father that it was normal to put the metal to the pedal when traveling on the roads of the zone.

We arrived in one piece to have a traditional German repast at an ancient guesthouse in the middle of Heidelberg. As dusk fell on the Neckar River, the hills were alive with Bavarians, and the passing night saw the lighting of the ancient castle along with a fireworks show à la Fourth of July. It was great to see the Toto family again, as we had a grand time that night. The next day, Bob was off with his parents to Italy and other countries of Europe. I was headed back to Wurzburg to my new assignment in the Special Services under the command of Captain Feelgood. Life looked great, time was passing, and no levies of IOBC classes loomed on the horizon. Hell, I had sixteen months to go. Wurzburg seemed like the ideal place to end my military career.

The Good Life of Wurzburg!

I reported to Captain Feelgood on Monday morning, and if there was a more relaxed commander in the army, I would have liked to have met him. The first thing he said to me was that the best thing that happened to me was taking my leave of Captain Uptight. Obviously, Uptight's reputation precedes him. The next thing he told me was that as long as I did what was ordered and necessary, I would have no problems from him. Feelgood was a career officer due to be promoted to a field-grade status, but his modus operandi was low-key, stable, and productive.

The good captain broke me in slowly with another experienced

AG (Adjutant General) officer who had been doing this for the last nine months. I was told to organize soldiers' activities, such as the Division tennis tournament, and to supervise the arrangements for incoming entertainment concerts being conducted throughout the various brigades and even at the division level. I was to coordinate the army's representation in promoting and executing these concerts with the division PIO (Public Information Office).

Hence it was inevitable that I would run into the formidable T. Couch. Oh, yes, dear folks, T. Couch had returned in all his loveable glory. Good old T had spent the last fourteen months grazing on the good life in Bavaria while cleverly concealing himself as an officer and gentleman. Of course, we all knew better! Couch was living the good life on the economy of West Germany. He lived off base and professionally did his duties in the competent manner of his rather competent demeanor. He wore the rank of first lieutenant and had the crossed rifles of an infantry officer. Indeed, he carried the rank and office. He had everyone fooled as he lived the life of ease and plenty. His attitude was reflected in the immortal words he said to me when he required that we play a pickup game of basketball: "Jeez, Geschke, we have to play at least one game in order to work off all the drinking and partying we've been doing." He was right, but to this day, this quote remains a "Couchism." As one can see, life was great as one turned the calendar to June of 1971. One couldn't get better duty in Uncle Sam's army as one counted down the days in Germany.

Couch Was the True Professional

One thing I began to realize was that T. Couch was good at doing his thing as public information officer. When the rock group Grand Funk Railroad came to do a concert for the Third Infantry Division, Captain Feelgood sent me on my first big assignment to coordinate the efforts of the Special Services with the Grand Funk Railroad advance publicity people of the band. As I headed into the conference room, lo and behold, here came T. Couch with pen and pad to record all the necessary propaganda for dissemination to the troops.

As an infantry officer of the line, this was all new to me, and I swallowed the communications front man's spiel in all its propaganda.

To him, Grand Funk Railroad was the hottest ticket in the realm of rock and roll. People were buying their albums by the thousands and they were constantly selling out audiences wherever they travel. This rant lasted a good forty-five minutes, in which this spokesman was asking for more than the usual backup and support as if this group were to be treated like the original Beatles. Once the meeting was over, I turned to Couch and stated that this group evidently deserved the royal treatment. Couch turned to me and said "Geschke, this is the typical bullshit they all say!" It was then that I knew that Couch was a pro in his job and deserved the respect of his professionalism as any other officer in Uncle Sam's army.

Lieutenant Tom Couch
In civilian attire by the Berlin Wall

Reality Sets In

I was getting into this staff job thing, and life looked good. I had my weekends free, and during my time in Wurzburg I traveled to Amsterdam and Berlin. I put my army career on an easy cruise control. About the middle of June, I was told to report to the G-1 shop. As I walked into the rather nice offices of the division personnel office, I had no idea that I was about to be given my orders for Vietnam. They read as follows: "Authorized leave and to report to Jungle Operations Warfare School, Fort Sherman, Panama CZ (Canal Zone) for training en route via Travis Air Force Base to PCS (permanent change of station) in RVN (Republic of Vietnam)."

The bastards finally got me! I scratched my head and tried to figure out why IOBC 8-70 was not levied and why IOBC 9-70 also escaped the Grim Reaper. All IOBC classes were numbered consecutively and in the protocol of the Vietnam era, all classes would rotate to Vietnam in numeric order. As I walked back to my office in a daze, I knew I had to call both Couch and Toto to see if they'd gotten their orders. Since Couch was located in Wurzburg, I called him first, and he said he'd received no such orders. As it turned out, T. Couch was the only vol-indef officer of IOBC 10-70 who was not levied for Vietnam.

Now I actually respect the army's decision on Tom's behalf. Couch was a true professional at his job. He was army trained for his position, and he was good at what he did. The next person I called was Toto. "Berlin. Dial your number." I did my rotary dial. Good old bouncing Bobo was in shock. I truly believe he thought he would escape "the Turk" and not take the trip to Southeast Asia. We had three more months in Germany, and it figured that when I finally got the army job of my dreams, Washington sent out its version of the Grim Reaper to piss on our parade!

Being in a division staff job was great, but my days were numbered. It was easy to get soft during this time span. With T. Couch, the parties were frequent and ran late. I was becoming softer by the day, and soon enough September came rolling around. It was time to leave the FRG (Federal Republic of Germany). I proceeded to sell my powder-blue VW. Where I was going, I wouldn't need it.

Back to the Lands of the Western Reserve

Finally, I boarded the bird in Frankfurt and headed due west to where else but Charleston, South Carolina. Within two days, I was home again in Cleveland, Ohio. It was great seeing the family and cruising around seeing old haunts and old friends. However, things were changing; most of my friends were married and had no time to entertain a single guy who would only be around for a couple of weeks. Toto and I got together on the shores of Lake Erie, where we bummed around and took in a Monday night football game, watching the Browns lose to the Oakland Raiders.

Before you knew it, my leave was over, and it was a time for a lecture from my father. The day before I was to leave for "jungle school," my father took me aside so my mother couldn't hear us. "Listen, son," he said, "in the year and a half you were in Germany, you only wrote to us ten or eleven times. Now you're going into combat, and you will write at least once each week! Also, in your letters, you will not mention any hardships or any talk of combat. Your duties will be strictly administrative. Do you understand me?"

General Carl F. Geschke had given his orders. All I could say was, "Yes, sir!"

Heading Toward Hades!

It was under these conditions that I proceeded to board the plane at Hopkins International Airport, destined for Charleston, South Carolina. Damned if I wasn't getting tired of that damned air base. With Panama, I was to return to the life of an infantry line officer. Boarding the plane on that October day, I thought, *Well, at least I'm not going directly to Nam.* As far as I was concerned, I was going to the tropical delights of Panama. How bad could that be? As was said in the *Laurel and Hardy* episodes, "This is another fine mess you've gotten me into!" Panama would prove to be one of my greatest challenges, and as I flew over the delightful Caribbean and looked down on the aqua green-blue shadings of the Atlantic, little did I know I was traveling through the gates of hell.

CHAPTER 14
A PATH BETWEEN THE SEAS:
HELL IS A VERY SMALL PLACE

There's a Classroom in the Jungle

Seasoning is what they said we needed,
As cattle on the range we followed
Onto the path between the seas.
The heat, the smell, and—God, yes—the bush
Makes for soldiers training in the jungle.
Fears are met;
Fears are negotiated.
Tell me, teacher, is this pain necessary?
How many before us have you helped?
How many are now dead?
Tell me, teacher, does this help us?
Does this make us better prepared?
Questions that can't be answered
Until we experience the sounds of guns.
Tell me, teacher, will this jungle help us
In the ventures of a war I dread?
—Richard C. Geschke, October 1971

Bob and I found ourselves in Charleston again, this time heading due southwest to take a flight to Panama City, Panama. The trip didn't take long, but as I looked down on the waters of the beautiful Caribbean, I knew that my destination would offer a lush tropical climate that would terrify 99.9 percent of the entire world's population.

After we landed, we took a bus trip along a winding road to the Atlantic side. It was here that we arrived at the site of the Gatun Locks, after which we crossed over the Canal onto the reservation that was Fort Sherman. As we traveled the isthmus, I noticed the thick jungle surrounding us. It was thick and menacing. My thoughts were that we just had to survive this extreme training of Jungle Operations Warfare School. One must remember that in the army, a tour of Vietnam was exactly twelve months. If one attended "jungle school," the two weeks spent in the jungles of Panama counted as time spent in the tour of duty for Vietnam. Between you and me, I would have rather spent the two weeks in Vietnam rather than Panama. In fact, they should have given us four weeks credit for the two weeks in this remote hellhole. So fifty-two weeks of a tour of Vietnam actually became a tour of fifty weeks "in country" and two weeks in "hell in a very small place." The jungle of Panama made the jungles of Vietnam look like kindergarten in comparison.

A Toto Moment

The Republic of Panama: Someone at the Pentagon felt that we needed seasoning before reporting for our duties in Vietnam. Their answer was Jungle Operations Warfare School in Panama. Since I had not received any line duty assignments, secretly I hoped that this training would prepare me for my duties in Vietnam. A contingent of infantry junior grade officers was sent, en masse, to Panama. While these officers were all infantry, they all had different backgrounds, especially me. Some were West Pointers, some were airborne/rangers, and some spent all their time in the field. I was unprepared for "jungle school." And let me tell you, it was hot.

Close to the Gatun Locks

As we arrived at Fort Sherman, we were assigned to concrete block quarters without air-conditioning, complete with latrine facilities with the smell of musty and acrid air. There was no breeze to speak of, and we were parallel to the Atlantic Ocean. In Fort Sherman, we could see the ocean vessels waiting on the Atlantic side to make passage through the Gatun Locks. The air was still as the side beach washed ashore, the weak pulsations coming from the Atlantic Ocean. The air was heavy, and the scene of the still ships at night seemed almost surreal in awaiting passage through the path between the seas built sixty years ago with the foresight of Teddy Roosevelt.

All we had was hot, thick air, which we had better get used to since this sultry air would also follow us to the Republic of Vietnam. Diagonally across from our billets, such as they were, was the officers' club annex, which had air-conditioning and which also housed the headquarters of the Jungle Operations Warfare School. Running parallel to the headquarters was an airstrip utilized by small fixed-wing aircraft and as a helipad for helicopters. For the next two weeks in mid-October, this was to be our domicile while not wandering around the jungles of Panama.

A Snake Eater's Welcome!

We were issued used jungle fatigues along with brand-new jungle boots. Jungle boots were different from the standard issue army boot or the upgraded Cochran jump boots. Jungle boots were constructed of canvas tops with extensive air holes along with rubber insoles with drainage plugs to let the water drain out from the base of the boot. Our head instructor was an airborne/ranger, jungle expert, pathfinder, and Special Forces veteran of two combat tours of Vietnam. His initial soliloquy to us was straightforward and blunt, and I quote, "Gentlemen, you will note that we have treated you as the officers and gentlemen that you are. We have not harassed you, nor have we made you uncomfortable. However, our mission is to teach you of the mysteries of the jungle. The jungle is your challenge, and the madder you get at the jungle, the more the jungle will kick your ass. We're here to show you how to tame the jungle and make it your friend. Please be attentive and follow our lead; we have learned how to live in harmony with the jungle."

Each day, we headed out to our classes, which introduced us to all aspects of the jungle. Look at a globe or world map and see just how close we were to the equator. In our training, we were never once put on ground military transport. There was only one way of getting there, and that was by foot. Hence the term of grunts to describe the affectionate slang term for an infantryman. If there is one place in the world where there is 100 percent humidity without raining, that would be Panama. By the time we arrived for our initial morning class, our fatigues were soaking wet. Quite literally, one could sweat out three pounds before the first class. I would say that on a normal day in the jungle, we were consuming three thousand calories and expending over six thousand calories.

In the FTX (field training exercise), or overnight training, we were easily burning off nine to eleven thousand calories. Working under such humid and tropical conditions required more energy and effort.

Did I Tell You about the Snakes?

Our classes ranged from how to deal with snakes to what is edible in order to survive in the jungle. We did fruit identification and learned what was edible and what was poisonous. There was the identification of animals okay for consumption, including iguana and monkey, and if you were lucky, you might find a stray chicken. In fact, one of the demonstrations had a Special Forces sergeant stroking a live chicken that was sitting comfortably perched in the sergeant's arm. Within sixty seconds that chicken was fully dressed and ready for the barbecue spit. Poor chicken! Furthermore, we had snake identification classes along with how to deal with insects along with a reminder to take our daily malaria pills. Many of our classes were actually in cleared areas built into the jungle, which we reached by graveled roads built by the engineers. In the middle of the day, the jungle was a place of many noises along with an enveloping mist that covered the low areas of the jungle floor. The Panamanian jungle was a triple-canopy roof that allowed some light in during the day, but once dusk fell on the jungle, it literally became pitch black.

> **A Toto Moment**
>
> The first three days were spent in "survival training." This encompassed learning to live off the jungle for food, water, and shelter. I do remember some of the training. We were shown how to kill a live chicken with only our hands, and how to skin and pluck the feathers. We were oriented on jungle foods, such as papaya, root plants that tasted like potatoes, and other assorted green vegetable root plants. I definitely remember the snakes. The army realized that most normal people have an inherent fear of snakes. Their answer to that was to display for us the most dangerous snakes indigenous to Panama, like the fer-de-lance, and to have us experience the "feel" of snakes. At the foot of the instructor were two burlap bags. He kicked one bag, and you heard the sound of rattlesnakes. He then removed a snake from the second bag. We were instructed to form a horseshoe-shaped line. Then, one by one, we were to grab the snake with our left hand, transfer it to our right hand, and pass the snake on to the next soldier in the horseshoe. I was about fourth in line, and believe me, I had a death grip on that snake. I am convinced to this day that the snake never made it past the sixth man, let alone to the end of the horseshoe, due to strangulation.

You Want Me to Rappel?

Our first real physical challenge was to learn the art of rappelling. As a backdrop to the rappelling escapades, I must inform the reader of the composition of just who made up this eclectic class of "future snake eaters." The majority of the class consisted of the vol-indef (voluntary indefinite time span) officers levied from IOBC 10-70, sans T. Couch. As a matter of note, this was the last IOBC class to be levied en masse for the Vietnam conflict. It was like a school reunion with officers who had served in Germany, CONUS (Continental

United States), Hawaii, and Alaska. We caught up on what we'd been doing and bemoaned the fact that we were all headed to the world's largest two-way rifle range. Also included in this class was a large contingent of Canadians who were fully charged and gung ho. The rest of the class was comprised of officers who volunteered for the school and others headed for their first combat tours. So as the full contingent of our jungle warfare class marched onto the grounds of the rappelling towers, we were about to face our first physical challenge aimed at building one's confidence. As we sat in the stands and listened to our instructors explaining to us all the proper uses of a rope and D-ring in rappelling down steep grades and cliffs, I looked at the towers we were to rappel down and rather smugly muttered, "Hey, this doesn't look so bad!"

Taming the Tower

At the end of the formal instruction session, we formed a single line at the base of the rappelling tower and climbed to the top of it. Once I was at the thirty-foot level and looking down, my tune as to how hard this would be changed instantly. I later found out that the fear factor for heights begins at twenty-five feet. So, you see, the army at times can train you in a proper manner; in this case, their motive was to scare the living shit out of me! It just so happened that Toto was behind me on the way up the tower. It looked like both of us were going to rappel side by side down the wooden tower. The modus operandi was that there were two ropes to rappel, and they were side by side. Neither Toto nor myself had ever volunteered for airborne or ranger schools. Our careers up until that point were firmly planted on the ground.

To tell you that I experienced trepidation would be putting it mildly, but I was an infantry officer and you can't act chickenshit. Out of the corner of my eye, I saw Toto clipping his D-ring, and to put it frankly, his face was ashen white. Well, scared or not, down we went, and once you learned how to trust the rope and D-ring, it was a piece of cake. Toto looked relieved as we hit the ground at about the same time.

Frozen Solid in the Jungle Heat!

Being sufficient veterans of the tower, back up we went for another rappel. Halfway up we were stopped because a captain was frozen with fear at the top of the tower and refused to go down. Toto and I climbed up the ladder for a second rappel, but the frozen captain blocked one lane. An E-5 (specialist fifth grade) was encouraging the captain to make good on rappelling downward off the tower. Steadfastly, he refused to make the descent. He was that scared! To my way of thinking, I would rather die than refuse to make the descent. As the scenario ran out on that tower for nearly an hour, I truly felt sorry for him. This particular action made me feel an embarrassment for him, which I could never live with if it happened to me. His fear overcame all his senses and created a hush over the whole tower area. Nothing at all was ever said again of this incident. All I remember saying to myself was, *Thank God it wasn't me.*

Finding Our Way in the Jungle

In our battle order of instruction, next we were instructed on land navigation in the jungle. The usual instruction of land navigation was given in the fine nuances of reading a topographical map and the use of the compass with the normal conversion of changing magnetic readings to topographical readings drilled into our heads. Prior to then, I'd been instructed in ROTC, IOBC, EIB, and the fields of Germany in Wildflicken and Grafenwoehr. Don't forget, I'd maxed most every course I'd been given. Had I had enough training? To me, Panama was the ultimate challenge. We were again instructed in the utilization of one-dimensional maps and taught to convert the images of the contour lines of the map as they would appear as pictured in our brains to visualize the three-dimensional focus of the actual lay of the land. In Panama, one must remember that the jungle was not flat. The jungle on the Atlantic side in the auspices of Ft. Sherman consisted of a rolling terrain. It was not flat. Oh, yes, dear reader, it was hilly. When we got into the actual day and night testing of our skills in the jungle terrain of Panama, we needed to remember the vegetation and animal life contained therein. When we considered all the aspects of what we had to endure, it's a wonder we didn't have any serious injuries.

We spent the rest of our first week in jungle school attending all sorts of other hygienic and other rather mundane classes. On Friday night came the visit to the aforementioned O-Club annex, with air-conditioning and all. As is normal in all such O-Clubs throughout the civilized world, we hoisted our brews to the instructors of jungle school and proceeded to get drunk! We were young, going to Vietnam, and above all, we had air-conditioning. So bugger off!

We were so tired as we dropped into our bunks in Fort Sherman on that Friday night, but we weren't respected a bit if we didn't travel into the port city of Colon on Saturday. Now, Toto and I were relatively experienced in dealing with the shady side of life in a foreign realm. Colon was an open city, and Bob and I had seen these cities in Mexico, Amsterdam, and Germany. To us, this was normal. Some of these other officers, well, they just ran wild. Within the week, several of these so-called officers and gentlemen were being inspected on daily sick call for a *short arm* inspection. All is fair in love and war! The fact remains that some of these officers and gentlemen were already married and had to deal with catching an infectious disease. I was single and unattached; they were married. Where were their brains? Go figure!

A Toto Moment

The first week was history, and Lord knows we stunk to high heaven. We removed our clothing outside the concrete barracks and burned our clothes. We had been discovered in a mock ambush, and because the "enemy" smelled us, we were doomed. We were rank. We took showers, hit the O-Club, got drunk, and slept until mid-afternoon Saturday. Geschke and I headed off to Colon to hit the bars. Remember that some of the soldiers had never been outside the United States and were not used to foreign cultures. Inside the bar, we were immediately assaulted by a henhouse full of ladies of the evening. They literally attacked us. At that time, I was a smoker, and the only recourse I had to free myself from these women was to burn their hands with a lit cigarette. Some of our aforementioned fellow soldiers availed themselves of the services provided. Later they would pay for their indiscretions when they contracted STDs. Fortunately, the army had developed a concentrated penicillin injection, and these troopers were out of service for only one morning. Leave it to Yankee ingenuity.

Panama was a free-trade zone, and we visited the local merchants. There were watches of all sorts, jewelry, and other offerings. I bought a Seiko watch for about twenty dollars. I had that watch for many years. Bartering was the order of business, and this place had it all. But good times have to end, and we had to move on. Just as in times of the British Empire, one finds American things throughout the globe, and Panama was no different. It makes sense since we were the nation that built the canal, so here we were.

We decided we were hungry, so Geschke and I found a VFW post close by. All the old veterans and old snake eaters were there. We ordered a fabulous surf and turf meal that was scrumptious. At the end of the meal and several drinks later, we were informed that our bill had been "taken care of." We tried to reciprocate to our benefactors but proved to be unsuccessful. We thanked them and left. We had no transportation and no inclinations to barhop. We called it a night among the "mules" of the Panama Canal.

In the Jungle, the Mighty Jungle!

The second week became the serious week, and we spent all our days as well as nights in the field. No more heading back to the concrete billets, where we didn't have air-conditioning but at least we had latrines and showers. The first day, we were tested on land navigation. We were broken into teams of four officers each and were given maps and compasses and told to hit three designated points in the jungle before 16:00 hours. Remember, this land navigation course was like no other. Although it was daytime, we were navigating thick jungle terrain, and don't forget that it was not flat. It was like traveling on a roller coaster, only your legs did the walking and took the abuse. The light that filtered through the triple canopy was like seeing at night in a room lit only by a weak sixty-watt lightbulb. The only way we could make headway was to have the point man hacking the thick underbrush with a machete; we carried four machetes because one machete would only last about two hours before it became too dull to cut any vegetation at all.

As we were hacking our way through the jungle, our mission was to hit three specified points. I took the responsibility of shooting the magnetic azimuths and guiding our group to our destination. Along the way, we were continually going up and down the terrain, sometimes coming across fast-moving streams. Whether going uphill or downhill, it was rather easy to lose your balance, and the first instinct was to grab the nearest vegetation available to help regain your balance and not fall on the jungle floor.

The "Black Palm"

In the Panama jungle, they had a plant that is only indigenous to that area of the world. It's called the "black palm," and if you brush against it or, as I did on several occasions, grab the plant in an effort not to fall, the pain is instant and unforgettable. The black palm is the vegetative equivalent of a porcupine. The plant is nothing more than a bundle of needle quills, much like the needles of a pine tree, only stiffer and longer. During the next several days, I hit the black palm by brushing up against it or while sliding down a hill, grabbing it in error to brake my fall. I hit the black palm so often that my hands were loaded with imbedded bits of black palm stalagmites that stayed in my skin long into my tour of Vietnam. In fact, I was still pulling out the remnants of the black palm in Phu Bai South Vietnam during the miserable monsoon rainy season.

Along with the dreaded stalagmites of the black palm, my arms looked like someone had come along and slashed them with a razor blade. Such was the brutal vegetation of the jungle of Panama and what it could do to your body. Along with the black palm, the air was thick with insects of all kinds, whether flying about or crawling on vegetation or the rotting jungle floor. This was like trying to negotiate the antics of a theme park's fun house. Take my word for it: this was no fun house. As we battled the jungle trying to hit our markers, our uniforms were becoming laden with our sweat, and the fatigues were literally shredding before our eyes. Even in the daylight in this little hellhole, life was no delight. Although we were struggling, we did make good time, and we hit our first marker by 10:00 hours. We decided not to rest but to head out to the next destination post haste.

The dreaded black palm, ouch!!

As we proceeded to the second marker, we come across a Canadian group headed in the opposite direction, also going to their second marker. Since they were going from where we came, I guessed they were headed for our first marker. I gave them a heads-up of exactly where to go, which they appreciated and reciprocated. As luck would have it, we hit our second marker before 12:00 hours. Talk about luck!

Known Points in the Jungle

At this point, let me tell you what the markers were. Each destination was an encampment with a fire barrel and first-aid equipment along with other jungle supplies, such as ropes, flashlights, machetes, and fresh water. These points were always contained on high ground, which made it easier for the wandering groups to see when seeking the coveted markers. The marker was manned by an NCO (noncommissioned officer) and acted both as the beacon marker destination and as the much-needed safety valve in case of emergency out in the hinterlands of a triple-canopy hell in a very small place. Also, we were relatively lucky that we were not lugging any backpacks, but in the army tradition, we were carrying the rather heavy armament of the M-14 rifle.

Again, we were training with 1950s' arms, which were not the rifles being used in Vietnam. A loaded M-14 combat weighs over twelve pounds. A loaded M-16 combat weighs nine pounds. What's the big deal, you say, when there's only a three-pound differential? Trust me that three pounds comes into play when navigating the rough terrain in Panama. We had hit two of the three markers by midday, so we decided to stay on the vegetative-free destination, and we wolfed down our c-rations. Within forty-five minutes, we were off to see the wizard of marker number three.

As the afternoon wore on, the machetes grew duller, our fatigues got heavier, it rained a monsoon shower of twenty minutes or so, and somehow, some way, we found marker number three. We happened to be near a gravel road of which I spoke of before, and we headed back to our base class area for evening chow. After eating, our teams were again formed, and the AIs (assistant instructors) were there to conduct a complete and thorough shakedown of all our uniforms and equipment. We were given specific instructions not to carry any flashlights or anything that would give off light, including matches. Sorry, guys, no smoking at night in the jungle. Now the real fun began!

A Toto Moment

Apart from the survival training, we had "physical training" to prepare us for our adventures. We had rappelling. As I said, these were people from extremely different backgrounds. Rangers and West Pointers were used to rappelling. Some, like me, were not. This was all new to me and didn't prepare me for the training later. During our first day of maneuvers in the jungle, our instructors told us to keep count of the number of canteens of water that we drank. He stated that the average person would drink twelve canteens of water per day. I thought he was crazy. I kept count, and in the course of the first day, I drank nineteen canteens of water. Believe me when I tell you that it didn't quench my thirst. All it did was replace the water my body had lost while sweating. Panama was like a sauna.

In the course of our romp through the jungle, we took turns on point (front man in the column). There were four-man crews slashing away at the foliage with the ever-present machetes. We traveled at the rate of one thousand meters (in army terms, one click) an hour. No wonder we offer our youth to the military establishment; an older person couldn't stand the physical demands of the jungle.

With 100 percent humidity, it was hard just to breathe under the triple-canopy jungle. I learned that cigarette smoke doesn't dissipate into the air. It hangs close to the ground like a seacoast fog. You could smell the smoke for hours. I would remember to tie my shoelaces tight around my boots at night so the snakes couldn't crawl inside. We slept in hammocks at night. You didn't sleep on the jungle floor in Panama.

I learned to stay away from paths at night, the favorite ambush site for snakes. I learned how to control some of my fears. At the end of the first week, we were to use our newly trained skills in rappelling. First we had to climb a mountainous peak, with personnel slipping down the slope throughout the climb. Once we reached the summit, we were to rappel down a one-hundred-foot waterfall, to awaiting safety personnel on the ground. I was scared out of my tree. At the beginning of the descent, we had to step upon a sill located about three feet below the precipice. As I tied myself with the rope and D-ring and prepared for the descent, I was in a panic. My thirty minutes of training did not give me the confidence to rappel the waterfall.

Suddenly, about three persons ahead, a captain refused to make the rappel. Nothing was said, but I saw the grimace in his body. Now it was my turn. I lowered myself down to the sill and prepared to rappel. Scared does not portray my deepest thoughts. Suddenly, Geschke, who was next in line, said "Toto, I've never seen you that color before." I laughed, and that broke the tension. I slowly lowered myself down the waterfall. Halfway down, I felt the cool water of the waterfall showering my face, and it felt great. I continued down the waterfall, even though in my ecstasy I was upside down. Thank God for those safety guys at the end of the rope!

Night Navigation in the Jungle of Fort Sherman, CZ

Once the shakedown was complete, we all felt like naked teenagers about to be sent to bed with no dinner. We were stripped down of all other equipment and all we had were the jungle fatigues and jungle boots along with a web belt and canteen and an army fatigue cap along with slinging our M-14s. No flashlight or matches were allowed. The only things offering any illumination were two strips of luminous tape affixed to the back of our utility caps. In this way, you were able to follow the man before you by watching the two small strips of luminous tape affixed to his cap. Again, this was a continuation of the daylight navigation course turned to finding three markers at night in the jungle confines of Fort Sherman CZ. As in daylight, all the markers were manned by NCOs, and in the thick of the night, their fires were lighted at high points all within the jungle interior.

As we disembarked from a solid gravel road and into the interior of the jungle, I experienced total darkness as I've never seen before. As in the daytime navigation, I again was chosen the group leader, and it was my responsibility to fix our magnetic compass position and guide our team to the designated markers. In order to pass the land navigation phase in jungle school, you had to hit four of six markers to pass. So all we needed to pass was to hit one marker in three. My responsibility was to guide all who were in front of me as to what direction to go. Terrain analysis was useless; all I had was my compass, so off we went. As difficult as it was during the day, at night we were literally like blind bats searching as if by radar to keep to the true azimuth as determined by me. Remember, the terrain was not flat as we stumbled blindly, trying to get to our destination.

During the process, I remember fixing our position every five minutes and stumbling down a hill and climbing up another hill. The insects were swarming every time we stopped. No amount of "bug juice" (insect repellent) would deter those damned pests! About every half hour, we would stop to rest in the blackness of the jungle, and some would do the unthinkable, which was to flop to the jungle floor and "rest their eyes." It was up to me to kick this group in the ass and continue. At about 24:00 hours, we hit our first marker. We passed! The NCO called in our safe arrival, and within ten minutes, we were off in search of our second marker.

Don't ask me why, but within the next two and a half hours, we hit our next marker with relative ease. It was about 02:30, hours and we had to hit our next marker by 06:00 hours. All I remember is that we decided that we need to rest for fifteen minutes at this high ground without the snakes and insects, and we fell asleep along with the marker NCO, awaking at 05:00 hours. I remember trying to suck out the black palm stubble, which I had acquired during our nocturnal escapades, from my hands. My hands and arms were torn to shreds. My uniform looked like I was a survivor of a holocaust camp.

As I was the first to get up, I shook the NCO awake and screamed to my fellow officers that it was time to move on to our rendezvous point, where we were to be collected and marched back to our next FTX exercise. The NCO pointed our group in the right direction, and we landed on a beach setting aside an old Spanish fort and the Atlantic Ocean. When we arrived, we flopped down and fell asleep; it was the sleep of the dead. Upon the horizon, there were more challenges, for we were the future "snake eaters" unplugged. It didn't get any easier.

Waking up to a Misty Scene

As I awoke in the misting scene of a beautiful area looking upon the ruins of an old Spanish fort nestled in the hills adjacent to the Atlantic Ocean, we were told that one of our fellow officers had lost his M-14 somewhere in the jungle during the night navigation course. The first rule of a soldier is that you always protect your weapon; you should never lose it. A sergeant first class shouted instructions that all classmates were to form a column to follow our branded officer sans M-14 to try to retrieve said weapon.

The groans and bitching even emanated from our always cheerful and gung ho Canucks, such was our disposition on that fine morning. Thank God the good airborne/ranger, Special Forces, pathfinder, snake-eating commanding captain saved our rather sorry asses by stating, "You sorry bastards should go back and find that weapon, but our training is on a strict schedule, and we have to move on." The good lieutenant who lost the weapon would end up paying for it, which I'm sure he cheerfully did to save him further embarrassment and further pain.

We proceeded down the waterway in an LST (landing ship tank)-type boat to the mouth of the Chagres River, where our instructors were planning other surprises and, for some, more pain and agony. As Bob had noted before, we had many officers of the airborne and ranger vintage, and to them, this training should have been at least more tolerable. As we proceeded to climb up a steep jungle grade, I did notice that some of these airborne/rangers were struggling just as much and in many cases more than Bob and I were. Once we arrived at the precipice of the summit, it suddenly dawned on us how we were to come back down.

A Waterfall in the Jungle

Now we realized why we were trained back on those towers to rappel down steep inclines. Much to our chagrin, this was a little more than a steep incline; this was a fast-moving waterfall these crazy snake eaters wanted us to rappel down. Toto was in front of me, and if I had had a camera, his pose would be used on a poster for a horror movie. I went down, and unlike Bob, I came down straight up, but I ticked off the AIs who were stationed on the bottom holding the rappel line as a safety precaution because I stopped in the middle of the waterfall to take a shower. I was filthy dirty, and the shower felt good. The AIs below were yelling at me to hurry down because I was causing a traffic jam on the top precipice of the waterfall.

Sliding over the Chagres River

Feeling a little more confident, we proceeded down the jungle path to the largest and biggest tree I have ever seen. We were told to climb up the staked ladder to a wooden floored area constructed on a major tree limb where a rope was strung across a rapidly moving Chagres River. All rangers knew how to do the slide of life, but it was done differently in jungle school, and if you didn't do it right, you could be in a whole world of hurt, quite literally. At ranger school, the slide for life was done as a slide, and at the far end of the waterway, the candidate would release himself from the rope and land in the water, finishing by swimming back to the embankment. This was not done at jungle school.

Their method of torture was to have the officer extend his arms into the loops of a rope, and the student would be pushed off and proceed rather rapidly on the wire until the rope was suddenly jolted by a large brake knot at the other end. We were instructed clearly that when the megaphone order of "Lift your legs!" was given, you were to extend your legs as if doing a leg lift to act as a braking mechanism to slow your descent. The extension of the legs gave a natural resistance to any forward movement. My heart was pounding fast, and I focused only on the brake knot, not looking down on the fast-moving river and not trying to think of just how high I was—with only two small ropes around my shoulders. As soon as I heard the megaphone blasting the orders, I lifted my legs and hit the rope at a smooth clip, exiting like a pro.

How One Airborne/Ranger Does the Slide for Life

Two slides later, Lieutenant AR (not using the real name to protect the guilty but as an abbreviation for airborne/ranger) didn't lift his legs and came crashing into the knot at full speed. When he did this, he looked like a man who had just been hanged, as in the old Western movies. He was strung up dangling like a doomed man. He had just dislocated both his shoulders, and this was Lieutenant AR's ticket for a permanent profile and no airline ride to the RVN (Republic of Vietnam). It just so happened that Lieutenant AR was a member of our IOBC 10-70 class; he was a chubby and rather erudite officer who decided to volunteer for airborne and ranger schools, which developed him into a rather gung ho officer of a line unit back in CONUS (Continental United States).

During his eighteen-month stateside tour, he met and married his sweetheart, and they had a child. His gung ho attitude turned to mush, and he was rather mundane and shocked when he received his orders for Vietnam. On this slide for life, Lieutenant AR was looking for the million-dollar wound, and he painfully got his wish. We proceeded to cross the Chagres River via wooden life rafts concocted of rope, wood, and ponchos. The river ran fast, and if you didn't pay attention, you could possibly let the current carry you away to the Atlantic Ocean. As we dragged our rather tired and ragged bodies farther, we continued our fun and games in jungle tactical exercises. Oh, the joy of it all!

A Toto Moment

With conquering the waterfall, the next test was climbing a one-hundred-foot ancient tree and placing a tear-shaped rope under my arms in which I hung suspended above and traversed river in the world. This contraption utilized a wheel sliding along a rope. The rope was secured to a large tree on the other side of the river. Once I reached the tower platform, I said to the NCO, "Kick me out fast or I'll freeze." He gladly accommodated. A knot in the rope brought you to a sudden and jarring stop. Some guys got separated shoulders from the jolt. I made it across the river and subsequently made a swim across the Chagres River on a man-made raft. I am a weak swimmer, but I did make it to the other side, come hell or high water.

Do you know how it feels to be tired? Rangers know two things when confronting ranger problems and tactics, and that is how to deal with no sleep and what it means to be hungry. In jungle school, we also experienced this, albeit for a much shorter duration. Our next phase was to conduct tactical operations in the jungle much like one would in the Republic of Vietnam. By this time, all of us were feeling the effects of the FTX (field training exercise) that we were experiencing. We had only two days to go, and I was determined to finish this course conducted in this hellish piece of the surface of the earth. I am known to have very weak ankles; they have the propensity to turn on a dime. During several instances in the day and night navigation course, I had turned my ankle several times as I gathered black palm in my hands while sliding down several embankments. This time, I traversed some uneven terrain in the open area of the jungle and fell to the ground in pain. The medic arrived and wrapped my ankle, utilizing cold ice packs to reduce the swelling. Within a half hour, I was evacuated on a jeep to the base hospital on the Atlantic side of the Canal Zone.

As luck would have it, the doctor was from Cleveland, and we had a great discussion of the happenings in Northeast Ohio. As he read the X-rays, he informed me that I had severely sprained my ankle and had a hairline fracture on the anklebone. I looked at him and said, "So how does this affect me on my orders to Vietnam?" He said it was not his decision, and that I would have to rest for the next couple of days. My days of being a snake eater had ended. Such a shame! After that, he told me to report to the army hospital at the presidio located just outside of San Francisco and await their evaluation of my condition.

Limping and Tossing my Crutches

To be frank, I was upset that I couldn't complete the last two days of the jungle school. I was given a set of crutches and told to go back to my quarters, such as they were, and rest. For two nights, I slept in the sweltering heat of the night in Fort Sherman, hearing the distant waves of the gentle Atlantic and the sounds of the air horns emanating from the ships about to traverse the Gatun Locks. When the class arrived, it was time to turn in our rags to be burned along with our rotten jungle boots. It was time to travel by bus back across the isthmus to Panama City.

Before I left the concrete domain of our rather humble furnishings of Fort Sherman, I took those crutches and tossed them onto the concrete siding of the barracks. I limped onto the shuttle with bouncing Bobo, and off we went—back to Charleston with Toto and on to the West Coast of America. I had a date with a doctor at the presidio, and deep down in my heart, I knew that my final destination was the Republic of Vietnam. Here I was, twenty-four years of age, well trained, and heading for the ultimate two-way rifle range. Where I was headed was in fact in the vernacular of a rifle range, only this range had targets that shot back.

CHAPTER 15
IN COUNTRY: THE REPUBLIC OF VIETNAM

Ho Chi Minh

You will kill ten of our men, and we will kill one of yours, and in the end it will be you who tire of it.

Ho Chi Minh

There I was on a plane, headed to where else but my favorite spot, Charleston Air Force Base. Until I started writing this memoir, I had forgotten how many times I'd visited the good people of South Carolina. Here I was with a bum ankle and both hands full of the remnants of the black palm, little reminders of my two-week "vacation" in sunny Panama. Once I touched base in Charleston, I made immediate connections for San Francisco. My primary destination was the presidio army hospital, and after getting a medical evaluation, it was on to Travis Air Force Base, where I was to disembark to the Republic of Vietnam. It turned out not to be a direct flight; I had to make a connection in Chicago at O'Hare Airport.

Toto was also headed to Vietnam via another that would take him to McCord Air Base and on to Vietnam. Toto and I said our good-byes in Charleston, and off we went on our great adventure. I landed at O'Hare and immediately sought out my connecting flight to San Francisco, where an unusual event took place—and one can't make up stories like this. It actually happened. As I was scurrying to find my connecting flight, all I remembered saying was, "Hi Bob. Where the hell is gate twenty-eight?"

Bob shrugged and said, "Where's gate thirty-four?" It was indeed a cosmic moment, and we continued on our separate ways. That's the last I saw of Bob until June 1972! I finally connected with my flight and went to the West Coast for the first time in my life.

I landed in San Francisco and grabbed a taxi to the presidio. I reported to the main desk, giving my 201 file (personnel records) to the attending administrator. I must have waited two full hours before I saw a doctor. He immediately ordered X-rays, which took another two hours. I had to wait another hour before I could talk to the doctor to analyze the results of the X-rays. He told me that I had a hairline fracture of my left ankle, and that my muscles were severely sprained. My mind said immediately, *No shit, Sherlock. Now what in God's name was I supposed to do?*

The rather young captain looked at me and said, "I see your orders are for service in Vietnam. Is that correct?"

In my mind, I said, *Yes, Your Stupidness*! But in reality, I said, "Yes, sir."

He proceeded to give me the standard army protocol in this situation. "Well, Lieutenant Geschke, I'm writing a profile [medical exception] for forty-five days of light duty. Remember to elevate your leg and rest it as much as possible."

At this point, I looked at the doctor and wondered if he was truly on the same planet I was, or perhaps being in the San Francisco area, he was partaking in the local drug culture so prevalent at that time! Obviously, he wasn't in the same army I was.

My mind was racing. The guy was an idiot. I couldn't report to a PCS (permanent change of station), to an infantry unit, stating that I was an invalid. Obviously, medical officers had no concept of the protocol of the line unit's mentality. I was an officer of the line, and as I proceeded out of the presidio, I crumpled up and threw in the trash the profile contained in my 201 file. As God is my witness, I wasn't going to Vietnam with sit-me-on-my-ass orders. I would be laughed out of the infantry. Make no doubt about it—I'm no hero, but deep down inside, I was scared as hell. In retrospect, it was a matter of personal honor. They told me I was an infantry officer, and by golly, I would proceed—even though I was scared shitless.

As I remember, it was getting late as I left the presidio—it was about 18:00 hours, and the flight from Travis was at 07:00 hours the next morning. All the bus lines were running their night schedules with extended hours and less direct runs to Travis. In need of some sleep, I spent thirty-five dollars to get to the replacement barracks at Travis at a decent hour. Imagine spending a fortune (thirty-five dollars was a lot of money in 1971) to go to Vietnam. Such was my state of mind.

As I entered the temporary billets at Travis, I was still hobbling and trying to extract the black palm from my devastated hands. I awoke at the joyful hour of 05:00 hours. I took a quick shower, shaved, and ate on the run, finally boarding the bird to Vietnam. I sat next to an E-8 (master sergeant) who was going to the RVN for the third time. His expertise was ordnance, and his specialty was EOD (explosive ordnance detachment). In the seventeen hours of air travel, the plane took us from Travis, with stops in Hawaii and Okinawa, with the final destination of Long Binh, I was instructed ad nauseam by the well-intentioned sergeant as to what to do in country in Vietnam. When we landed there, I got off the bird, and unlike most veterans of Vietnam, the heat did not affect me, for my last duty station was in the jungles of Panama. What I do remember was the smell—which was like incense—of the sweet and sickening thick air that permeated much of South Vietnam.

As I entered the auspices of the Ninety-Second Replacement Battalion, I was introduced to an E-6 who was welcoming all of us to the Republic of Vietnam. He immediately explained to us that we were to exchange all our US money for MPC (military payment certificates). Oh, the joy of it all as I gave the clerk real US greenbacks in exchange for the Monopoly money that was MPC. The use of this currency was changed frequently in RVN to prevent black market activities with US currency. This was the economic domain of Vietnam. Also, we were issued several sets of brand-new jungle fatigues along with our duffel bags and jungle boots. All the officers immediately went to the local Vietnamese tailors to have any other badges sewn on. In my case, I had the EIB sewn onto my jungle fatigues.

We'd landed in Long Binh in the early morning, about 03:00 hours, and by 08:00 hours, we were given a "dream sheet" on which to indicate where we wanted to be stationed. The choices included the 1st Cavalry Division, the 23rd Infantry Division, and the 101st Infantry Division, along with the Support Commands of Saigon, Da Nang, and Cam Ranh Bay. I selected all the support commands. Guess what—they gave me Da Nang.

At this time, another lieutenant, an IOBC 10-70 graduate, was also checking the roster. He was headed to Da Nang with me. The lieutenant's name was Tom Stickney, a graduate of Yale (class of 1969). Tom also went vol indef, and like Bob and me, he was stationed in West Germany with the Eighth Infantry Division. Being an Ivy League graduate, Tom gave the appearance and the demeanor of a well-bred East Coast Brahmin. He was slight of build, stood approximately five feet nine inches, and wore wire-rimmed glasses. He looked the studious type, like a college professor. As I would find out over the next two months, Tom was an organizer and problem-solver extraordinaire. Without Stickney, my mission in Phu Bai might never have turned out the way it did. So there we were, ready to take a plane ride to Da Nang. Stickney was following the same route as I had taken with leaving Germany in September, taking leave, and also attending Jungle Warfare School. As we boarded the C-130, we started to converse about just where the army was sending us as our final destination.

Freeze Frame: The Vietnam War, Circa 1971

At this point of the story, it's time to delve into the history of what was transpiring in Vietnam in 1971. The ongoing struggle that was the Vietnam War had been going on since the French fought the Viet Minh for eight long years after the end of WWII. Vietnam was part of the colony of French Indochina, a reign that lasted from 1887 until the fall of Dien Bien Phi in March of 1954. The settlement of the French Indochina War produced the results of the Geneva Conference, when France relinquished any claim to the territories of the Indochinese peninsula. The settlement divided Vietnam in two, with the Communist North Vietnam and a democratically elected South Vietnam. From this point forward, the United States became a prime player in this region as part of the Cold War concept of détente. Almost immediately, Eisenhower had military advisers sent to South Vietnam to assist the fledgling South Vietnamese Armed Forces.

When Kennedy was elected, he increased the military assistance and the number of advisers during the struggles of President Diem, who was leading a corrupt regime and whose armed forces were completely inept in fighting the Vietcong insurgency. During JFK's short presidency, the United States was behind the coup to oust Diem from leadership. The coup took place, and Diem was assassinated. During this time span, more advisers were sent to Vietnam, and the concept of the Green Berets was born.

After the assassination of JFK, Johnson increased the military involvement to the point of staging a false attack of a US warship in the Gulf of Tonkin incident. By 1965, the first military units were fully engaged in combat. From that point on, it was a steady stream of US Army and Marine units conducting search and destroy operations in all areas of South Vietnam, from the Mekong Delta to the DMZ (demilitarized zone). In time, General Harkin left the command of Vietnam, and General Westmoreland took over, immediately requesting a boost in the troop commitment, which by 1968 reached over five hundred thousand. In January of 1968, the NVA and Vietcong conducted a coordinated attack on all the major cities of South Vietnam, which is the well-known Tet Offensive. Although the attacks were major disasters to the North Vietnamese, they did in fact put doubt in the public persona of the war as it played out its horrific scenarios each night on TV screens throughout the United States. Walter Cronkite did a special personal report from the fields of Vietnam, which in essence was questioning our mission and purpose in this faraway land.

Criticism escalated, and the antiwar movement was gaining purpose and momentum. President Johnson was fully committed to "winning the war at all costs," so much so that his poll numbers took a drastic dive, and before the 1968 Democratic National Convention, he announced "with a heavy heart" that he would not seek reelection for the presidency. That year, 1968, was the key year in the turn of events that would ultimately lead the United States to seek a negotiated peace settlement. This effort would take over four years, and to the draftees and officers who were still fully engaged in combat, the negotiations were nothing but talk.

By 1971, during President Nixon's watch, the process of Vietnamization started to occur. Vietnamization was the turning over of the combat responsibilities to the ARVN (Army of Vietnam) so that in theory, over a matter of time, all combat would be the responsibility of the South Vietnamese. Along with the switch of combat duties, the United States fully outfitted all armed forces of the Republic of Vietnam with all the latest equipment.

As I arrived in November of 1971, more than fifty percent of the combat troops in South Vietnam were ARVN. However, the army had one major division in each of the four military districts of South Vietnam. At that time, enemy activities were generally pointed at the ARVN units. The Vietcong at this time did not want any major confrontations with US Army units. The enemy was smart enough to know that if they let Uncle Sam alone, Uncle Sam would eventually go away under Vietnamization. However, this did not mean that the enemy would not ambush or not have small-unit engagements. In 1971, US military KIA (killed in action) averaged forty-three GIs a week. Things were still very serious and dangerous in the RVN.

Da Nang: The Repo Depot Was a Swamp

Remember the TV show *M*A*S*H*? Remember the living facilities of Hawkeye Pierce and Trapper John in that makeshift tent? Well, the "swamp" of *M*A*S*H* lore was a palace next to what Stickney and I had to endure for a four-day period. Lieutenant Stickney and I reported to the repo depot in Da Nang, where the clerical facilities were shacks made of plywood, painted OD (olive drab), and there were sandbags three-quarters of the way up the outside walls as shrapnel barriers in case of enemy fire. Things were rather primitive, and to make matters worse, the northern end of South Vietnam was in the midst of their five-month monsoon season. When we reported to the auspices of the clerical domain of the Da Nang repo depot, we were told that we were to be quartered inside a tent facility about two hundred yards away and to wait there until we received our PCS orders. We were also told where the facilities were and the location of the mess hall. These facilities were rather primitive but had all the necessary amenities to live halfway civilly.

Vietnam's Class System

At this point, we must pause in the story and explain the soldiers' living conditions in the Republic of Vietnam, circa 1971. As far as I know, no one has classified the living facilities as they were during the Vietnam conflict. I think it's prudent to do so in order to give the reader a sense of class structure and of just how one spent a tour of duty in a combat zone. From time immemorial, the soldier always tries to secure the most comfortable facilities while enduring the inconvenience of what transpires during hostilities. Vietnam was no different, and below are the major classifications of military installations as they existed in the Vietnam conflict:

Classification 1: The top-of-the-line living facilities were mansion-like houses for embassy officials and general staff officers in the Saigon and Long Binh areas. All the amenities of home and the posh living of, say, the Washington elite were fully in evidence. This included a full complement of servants and the necessary transportation vehicles that were at the full disposal of these officials. Air-conditioning, running water, and full electronic communication along with the full protection of military police and security were fully used in these installations and houses. The offices of the staff were also fully complemented, and while the staff were housed in less posh facilities, they had permanent homes that were much like any middle-class home in the United States. This was all top of the line; you couldn't live any better than this in the RVN. The normal dress attire in this atmosphere was Class I TWs (tropical worsteds).

Classification 2: On the second rung were district officials living in areas such as Da Nang, Cam Ranh Bay, and Saigon; these were general officers or officials of high rank. These domiciles were either permanent homes of middle-class structure or lavish mobile homes. These facilities had hot running water, electricity, and full plumbing. The kitchens were manned by mess hall sergeants or civilian chefs. The support staff had air-conditioning along with plumbing and were housed in permanent structures, which means either brick or concrete block. The normal uniform was highly starched jungle fatigues, and the jungle boots were highly polished. Local Vietnamese mama-sans and papa-sans maintained the clean uniforms and shined boots. All of these structures had central air-conditioning or window air conditioners.

Classification 3: This classification was a semi-permanent site that contained buildings made of plywood, and each building was sandbagged to protect personnel from incoming fire. Most buildings were not air-conditioned, but some were. Electricity was provided by generators that were maintained by either quartermaster or engineer units. Engineers purified the water, and each compound had its own pipeline for providing the water supply. There were plumbing and bathroom facilities. All hooches were made of plywood and sandbagged. There were mess halls with ice and electricity. At the end of each row of hooches were sandbagged dugouts to go to in case of incoming rockets. The uniforms were clean and often consisted of helmets, bush hats, boonie hats, and flak jackets.

Classification 4: This was where a soldier started to "slum it." All buildings were constructed of plywood painted olive drab and sandbagged almost to the roofline. The only plumbing that existed was in the mess hall, which did have purified water. The entire compound had electricity provided by several running generators operated by company personnel as part of their guard duties. There was no plumbing, such as toilets or running water for shaving. Shaving was done with rainwater only. Showers were taken with rainwater only. There were no toilets, only outhouses. All solid excrement was dealt with by Vietnamese "shit burners," who utilized diesel gas in barrels to burn off the waste. Located at strategic spots throughout these compounds were sandbagged shelters dug into the ground— to be used during incoming rocket attacks. These conditions were primitive, and one never got the sense of truly being clean in such an environment, especially during the rainy monsoon season. Uniforms in these areas were often somewhat dirty, whether one was an officer or EM. The boots may have been brushed shined but within the first hour, they would be dirty, and in the rainy season, they would be soaked. After about two weeks, the canvas uppers would start turning brown with jungle rot. Rank was seldom worn in the field and was somewhat optional at the base.

Classification 5: These were firebases where line units were placed on high visual points with clear lines of fire along with an artillery battery and mortar platoon for indirect fire support. These were infantry and artillery facilities where the personnel used dug-in trenches with sandbagged protection. There was no running water, and the electricity was generator induced. These sites were in blackout at night and ran constant patrols into their area of operation. This was the primitive life of a field soldier. Slit trenches were used for "facilities," and hot meals were usually brought in. Some firebases had the ability to generate hot meals on site. Rotating companies shared the night watch on the perimeter NDP (night defensive perimeter). All night long, the artillery and mortar teams would be firing H&I (harassing and interdicting) rounds. In Vietnam, it was at the basic firebase level where uniforms were no longer uniforms in the military definition of the term. Bush hats and boonie hats were in vogue at the firebase; however, if an officer was worth anything, he would insist that his grunts wear the helmet and liner out in the field. Even the helmet camouflage lining was used as an expression of individual thought, with "short-timers'" calendars etched on the lining, Short-timers' calendars were penned calendars which usually showed thirty days in numbers with Xs marked on days already past. On extremely sunny days, grunts at the firebase would be shirtless when performing their duties. The uniforms were generally dirty and in many cases never cleaned. They would just be thrown away and new ones issued. Boots probably lasted anywhere from two weeks to a month if you were lucky. Rank was seldom worn at firebases.

Classification 6: This was the field—no plumbing, no electricity, no hot meals, no running water. At night, the unit secured high ground and formed an NDP (night defensive perimeter) with overlapping fields of fire and OPs (forward outposts) to secure early defensive warning. The usual field operation was an average of one week at a time, usually conducted at company and platoon levels. Each night, these NDPs were hastily dug in and cleared for adequate fields of fire. Uniforms were much like described in Classification 5; however, most GIs wore flak jackets, and if it was especially hot and humid, it wasn't unusual for the jackets to be abandoned in the jungle.

So as one can see, the living conditions in country varied a lot and indicated a wide variety of experiences. The above classifications are in no way indicative of the only types of facilities or living conditions in Vietnam. In fact, many GIs had a mixture of several of the above classifications in their own domains of the RVN. These classifications are meant as a guide to the reader to provide a sense of how one negotiated and conducted operations in Vietnam.

Living in the Swamp

Stickney and I went to the mess hall for dinner. As officers still technically traveling to our next PCS (permanent change of station), we had to pay for our meals. In Vietnam, once an officer was assigned a unit, he no longer drew a subsistence allowance and was directly fed without charge by the army. Since Stickney and I were yet to be assigned, we still had to pay. Neither of us had been paid for two months, and we wouldn't be paid until we were permanently assigned. We chowed down and went through the drenching monsoon rains that, along with the high winds, were pelting our poor tent where we were to spend the night. Wooden pallets served as our flooring, and we could actually hear the water below the pallets as it ran through our tents. Our beds were standard army cots along with those wonderful abrasive, itchy army blankets.

Did I mention the mosquitoes? Mosquitoes were there in abundance, and they liked Yankee blood all night long. We had just started to take our malaria pills, and it was a good thing that we did. Between the hard rainfall, the running water, the itchy army blankets, and the damned mosquitoes, I somehow made it through the first night. Both of us were welted red with mosquito bites, and I doubt we each got two hours of sleep. We went to morning chow and waited; we went to lunch and waited; we went to dinner and waited. We tried to sleep for the second night, but the rain and mosquitoes did us in again. My wallet was getting thinner, and the only thing that saved our sanity was the fact that they did have hot running water and we did take showers. This continued ad nauseam through the third day. My patience was running thin.

Finally, I told Stickney, "I've had enough of the bullshit!" I took it upon myself to visit those nerdy desk jockeys in Da Nang.

I went in, spoke to a staff sergeant, and asked him if his office had a problem in assigning Stickney and me to a permanent change of station. The good sergeant started to hem and haw, and I quickly put it this way, "Sergeant, you have two choices: you either send us back stateside or assign us a unit now!" He looked at me as if I had three heads; the mosquitoes had bitten me so much that the swelling probably did make me appear to have three heads on my body.

"Look," he said, "we were trying to get you to an infantry unit, but there are no officer openings. I'm in contact with a maintenance unit that needs combat engineers; I'm looking for their approval.

I looked at the sergeant and said distinctly, "Today, Sergeant, today."

Within three hours, we had orders to report to Phu Bai, which was located due north of us, south of Hue. The unit to report to on our orders was the Sixty-Seventh Maintenance Company. I looked at Stickney, shrugged my shoulders, and said, "Why on earth would a maintenance company need combat engineers?"

Stickney said, "Don't ask questions. At least we get a PCS and out of this rat hole." The sergeant immediately apologized to us, saying that the Chinook chopper going to Phu Bai was full, and that we would have to wait until 11:00 hours the next morning to travel via a C-130.

Another night in the tent, but I never felt comfortable or safe being in a Chinook ever since I was in one back at Ft. Benning in 1969. They called them eggbeaters. So just as well; a C-130 would be smoother and faster. During that evening and into the night, the winds and rains were the worst I'd ever seen, even to this day. It was indeed a torrential typhoon hitting up against the South Vietnamese coast along the South China Sea. Dear reader, you have never seen so much rain in your life!

Phu Bai Is All Right!

After surviving a terrible night trying to sleep through a major typhoon, things started to actually clear up. There still was a light drizzle as we headed to Da Nang Air Force Base. We headed to the C-130 that would take us to Phu Bai. As we boarded and took off from Da Nang, I mentioned to Tom that it seemed as if the levy of IOBC 10-70 was a lark that should not have been made. It seemed that all the career and West Pointers were clamoring to get their tickets punched for combat duty in Vietnam. In truth, time was getting short, and with the implementation of Vietnamization, the portal to "combat experience" was going the way of the dodo bird. Career officers needed to have combat experience in their 201 files or they would be at a serious disadvantage as they tried to progress through the ranks of a military career. Our long delay in Da Nang was the result of an overabundance of junior officers of the infantry persuasion "sent to the RVN". They didn't know what to do with us. Nevertheless, we landed in Phu Bai, where it was raining.

The Mission Statement

We were met by an E-5 (specialist fifth grade) who drove us to battalion support headquarters to meet Lieutenant Colonel F. We waited in the orderly room for several minutes, discussing just what in the world we would be doing in this rather remote section of South Vietnam, where the rain and clouds continued the onslaught of the meteorological realm, providing a rather somber and soggy existence. Tom and I went directly to meet Lieutenant Colonel F. The first words spoken by this career ordnance officer were, "Gentlemen, I see both of you are infantry officers."

I thought, *No shit, Sherlock. Please tell me something I don't know.*

He turned his eyes directly to us and pulled no punches. "I've got one month left here, and I'm on the colonel's list for promotion. General Sweeney has charged me with a most important mission that I am delegating to you to accomplish on or before December 25, 1971. That mission is to complete the eastern fortifications on the Phu Bai ASP (ammunition supply point) within the aforementioned timetable."

I immediately looked to Stickney, who blurted out, "Sir, we're not combat engineers; we are trained for the line duties of the infantry."

Lieutenant Colonel F turned his eyes to me and without hesitation stated, "I couldn't get an engineer officer, so I told Da Nang to grab me two lieutenants of the infantry persuasion. Why? Simple. In my army career I've found infantry officers to be the most flexible and the most trainable. Yes, I would have preferred one or even two engineer officers, but my deadline grows short. Vietnamization is the buzzword, so you guys are my ticket for a promotion and also a DSC (Distinguished Service Cross)."

Only in the Army!

I looked at the rather cool, calm, and collected Lieutenant Stickney, who immediately said, "Yes, sir!" Oh, great. What the hell did we know about defensive fortifications. But Stickney was Ivy League, and he must have had a plan in that rather astute brain of his. Lieutenant Colonel F indicated that with the successful completion of these fortifications, multiple units would be stood down and their colors returned to stateside with the accomplishment of our mission. He indicated that the accomplishment of the mission was to be determined by an inspection of the brigade commander of Phu Bai of the ARVN (Army of the Republic of Vietnam).

I looked at Tom and shrugged my shoulders. I turned to Lieutenant Colonel F and said, "Sir, we have no conception of what we are to do or accomplish. Do we have anyone to guide us as to how we are to proceed as far as daily operations and logistics needed to accomplish this mission? "

"No problem, Lieutenant. I have a sergeant first class from an engineer battalion; he'll guide you in all aspects of your mission. I've already briefed him just this very morning. He'll be at the ASP at oh eight hundred hours sharp."

The good lieutenant colonel also briefed us as to the reinforced platoon of short-timers assigned to us to complete the mission. He stated that the men all had less than three months left in country, and that they all were with either combat units that had been sent back stateside or support units that no longer existed due to the Vietnamization. Stickney and I were told where to hold our formations the next morning; we were to organize this ragtag compilation of humanity into a cohesive and functioning unit.

We walked out of the rather comfortable offices of Lieutenant Colonel F and headed to the orderly room of the Sixty-Seventh Maintenance Company to report to Captain Farmer, who was to be our administrative leader, only for "morning report" purposes. In essence, we both worked for Lieutenant Colonel F, whose boss was General Sweeney, the commander of the Da Nang Support Command.

Into the Thick of It

We were shown to our quarters, our home for the next two months. In the above installation rating, this place in Phu Bai would be Classification 4. As I found out, the mess hall was first rate, and it was managed by an E-6 who performed daily miracles for the troops. In my twenty-eight months of service to Uncle Sam, I would consider that mess sergeant a true chef. His cooking was like eating my mother's food. High praise, indeed! Stickney and I squared away our equipment and were issued flak jackets and weapons. We had the chance to meet most of the men assigned to our platoon. Throughout this time, we noticed that the rain did not cease. During the rainy season, one never saw the sun, and while the rain may slow to a drizzle, it would continue nonetheless.

The next morning, Stickney and I were at the mess hall by 05:30 hours. The mess sergeant never closed the hall; it was always open 24/7. If you needed a quick cup of joe, it was there, along with extra goodies, such as rolls and cookies and crackers. The compound was indeed a twenty-four-hour operation, and infantry security was guarding the outlying perimeter every night. By daybreak, the combat engineers were on their daily routine of sweeping all the roadways of mines and booby traps. By daylight, even in the monsoon season, the skies were alive with the steady *whop, whop, whop* of the incessant choppers that were coming and going as if the skies were part of a bee colony.

Also, much to my immediate annoyance, just down the road was an artillery battery that fired H&I fire all night long. I had a hard time sleeping that first night, but as time wore on, I quickly found out that I couldn't sleep unless I heard that steady cadence of outgoing ordnance each and every night. After morning chow, we headed to our assigned assembly point, took attendance, and headed the men to three deuce and a half trucks to trek to our assigned location by the ASP (ammunition supply point). We were met by a sergeant first class who wore the patch of the 101st Airborne Division.

The Scope of the Mission

The good sergeant had a truck full of equipment and tools for the platoon to utilize. The first thing he did was introduce himself and give us an overlay of just how he was going to organize the training. He informed us of the exact specifications we were to meet in order to turn over the ASP to the ARVN. Listed below was the exact protocol used for the two days of training:

> The specifications for the east fortification of the Phu Bai ASP were a distance of approximately one kilometer from the end of an old French minefield to the front gates of the ASP. The materials to be used in the construction of these man-made barriers were concertina wired rolls, concertina wire strands, three-foot engineer stakes, four-foot engineer stakes, and six-foot engineer stakes. The order of fortifications from the outside facing the enemy to the inside of the secured ASP was as follows:

1. The three-foot engineer stakes were sledgehammered to the ground at four-foot intervals four feet in front of the four foot stakes were sledgehammered into place.
2. Concertina wire strands were contained on one-hundred-foot reels manned by two men with leather gloves who

proceeded to wire the three-foot engineer stakes to each other. They would also do this with the four-foot stakes. Another wire strand team would be crisscrossing between the three-foot stakes and the four-foot stakes to create a low-lying concertina apron barrier.

3. There were multiple teams of sledgehammer groups responsible for hammering in the three-footers, four-footers, and six-footers. All sledgehammer teams wore leather gloves to prevent blisters (in theory). All staking was started in advance of laying down any concertina wire and concertina wired rolls. In effect, think of this construction as the laying of the engineer stakes is the same as the iron framing of a building structure; without this base skeletal foundation, no barrier can be built.

4. The order of protocol called for staggered starts, and the order was done as follows for the entire kilometer. I failed to mention previously that this fortification was literally built in a swamp at the depth of about two and a half to three feet. Remember, it was raining all the time, sometimes so heavily that I couldn't see all the teams that were staggered on the line. Fine weather for a duck! Below is the line of fortification built from the outside (enemy) to the inside (secure ASP):

5. Low-lying wired apron, four feet

6. Four-foot wired fence with concertina strands

7. Three rolls base concertina wired rolls. Second level, two rolls concertina wired rolls. Third level, one roll concertina wired rolls.

8. Four-foot wired fence with concertina strands

9. Three rolls base concertina wired rolls. Second level, two rolls concertina wired rolls. Third level, one roll concertina wired rolls.

10. Six-foot wired fence with concertina strands

11. Four rolls base concertina wired rolls. Second level, three rolls concertina wired rolls. Third level, two rolls concertina wired rolls. Fourth level, one roll concertina wired.

12. Four-foot wired fence with wired concertina fence
13. Three rolls base concertina rolls. Second level, two rolls base concertina rolls. Third level, one roll base concertina roll.
14. Four-foot fence with concertina fence
15. Low-lying apron, four feet

Remember, all these specifications, as laid out by the ARVN, were to be done during the monsoon season in a swamp. I looked at Stickney, who was as cool as a cucumber. It was time to put our ragtag outfit of twenty-five troopers to the test.

The next several hours felt like watching Laurel and Hardy moving a piano or The Three Stooges painting a home. If my life depended on these guys to do the job, I would have to call Dr. Kevorkian, such was my state of mind. Stickney, on the other hand, took this training exercise as an intellectual puzzle to solve. In a matter of two days, the troopers tried to replicate the action of the good sergeant first class, but in all instances, they failed in their attempts. In the first two days, we went through fifty sledgehammers. The simple reason was that they were used wrong and frequently missed the engineer stake targets. In baseball, it's called a swing and miss, a strike! My guys were swinging for the fences and missing.

It was time to show our "sluggers" to hit for singles and play "small ball." In other words take shorter and more accurate sledgehammer swings. It actually took six weeks to get it through the brains of these guys, but in the seventh week, we had covered 25 percent of our objective and finished the job! After two days, we were still stumbling and bumbling along, but Stickney and I knew the basic ropes, and it was time to move forward with this most essential mission. As our teacher left to go home from his second tour, it was our turn to step up to the plate and follow an essential mission through to its end. Not many officers were present to accomplish such a key mission.

Getting Ready to Turn off the Lights in Phu Bai!

This mission had everything to do with Nixon's concept of Vietnamization. Even in the short time that I was in country, I knew that we didn't belong in a place of civil strife about which we

Americans should have no say. The concept of the "domino effect" was a misguided theory. In effect, both Stickney and I were reversing our participation in this "civil war" and aiding in our termination of fighting a war that could never be won. Facts are facts: we had an invalid mission statement that would essentially have no bearing whatsoever on the Cold War. Stickney helped me in my main mission to aid other Americans in turning off the lights in Phu Bai and heading for home. At that time, the war was but a concept of saving face. Such a civil war could never be won by an outside party. Family is family; all the North Vietnamese and Vietcong did was wait it out. The negotiations were accomplished, and the United States was nothing but an observer. We won the battlefield, but by 1971, in our hearts, we knew we'd lost the war.

CHAPTER 16
PHU BAI IS ALL RIGHT!

In life, there are few times when all the stars and constellations are aligned right, but even though you have to endure hardships, everything turns out right in the end, and you accomplish all the goals you set out to do. Such was the saga of the forthcoming scenario that I'm about to reveal. According to Hanoi Hannah, Phu Bai was all right. Who was Hanoi Hannah, you ask? She was the radio voice of Hanoi and the communist regime, trying to persuade us that we were nothing but mere fodder in serving the capitalistic regime in gaining profits and preserving the upper classes of the socioeconomics of so-called democracy. Each night, Hanoi Hannah would foretell to the GIs where the Vietcong would attack or rocket on that particular eve. During my time in Phu Bai, Hanoi Hannah would always say, "Phu Bai is all right!"

In my two-month duty of Phu Bai, Hanoi Hannah was indeed right; we were never attacked. Straight down the road from our Class 4 facilities, such as they were, was a firebase with an artillery battery housed in Class 5 facilities that had the mission of firing H&I fire from sundown to early dawn each and every day. From the first evening until the time I left Phu Bai, that battery serenaded me every night. The cadence was in measured tempo, and I drifted into la-la land each night as the battery inflicted pain and suffering to the indigenous VC (Vietcong). It was amazing to me that the Vietcong never retaliated. Phu Bai had been an area of extended conflict during the Tet Offensive in 1968 and into 1969. Along about 1970, this area became a limbo or a neutral area where the VC did not extend their way of life or intentions directly on Americans and the ARVN. Phu Bai essentially became an area of mutual détente, a place to watch for booby traps, where one wondered when the VC or North Vietnamese were going to destroy the ammunition supply point.

The Cadence Takes Hold

Our first day without our combat engineer NCO proved to be an exercise in learning who was to do what—and just how Stickney and I were to utilize our leadership abilities. Before going into this scenario, I want to give you a visual picture of just where we were, and in doing so, show you what our task was and how we proceeded. The ASP was a man-made series of concrete bunkers built into an elevated mound of earth, much like city dumps would be constructed in landfill areas throughout the United States. An intricate system of dirt roads used by heavy-duty vehicles to transport ammunition in and out was part of the elaborate system. The system carried the vehicles up the elevated slopes to each concrete containment area built into the earth. The ASP was a circular perimeter of about three-quarters of a mile in circumference at the base of the containment.

It was a huge facility, and if not protected properly, it would be an open invitation to the enemy as a target of destruction. The location of our fortification building site was at the base in front of the ASP, on the eastern end of the facility. The area was in a swamp setting, running parallel to a dirt road about half a kilometer away. Our work area started on the south side, adjacent to an old French minefield. Looking from the first tier road of the ASP down on our worksite, we were building from the south to the entrance gate located one kilometer north. I supervised this construction, which was going from right to left. Our base point was to set up our command post in the lead truck, where we had our communications. We used three trucks to transport the troops and supplies back and forth to the work site and Camp Eagle.

Our supply train to Camp Eagle consisted of securing the necessary concertina, engineer stakes, sledgehammers, and work gloves. The Camp Eagle G-4 was the major supplier of our mission.

146

The road to Camp Eagle was located to our west, along a dirt road, which in the monsoon season was a muddy trek that we didn't dare travel down until the engineers cleared the road of any mines or booby traps every morning. It became apparent from the beginning that Stickney was the detail man; he would run the logistical end of the operation. His job was to make sure that we had the materials and tools to continue operations uninterrupted. He took care of the requisitions and coordinated all the transportation throughout the day. My job was to oversee the building of the fortifications and to deal with the day-to-day personnel problems and discipline.

At the beginning, Stickney had his routine down pat; I, on the other hand, was struggling with finding the right man for the right job. Certain personalities clashed as I broke the twenty-four men into eight teams of three men each. It took me a whole week out in the marsh patties of Phu Bai to find out the right combinations to move ahead in our objective. As my men stumbled and bumbled about, breaking multitudes of sledgehammers in their attempts at driving in engineer stakes, missing only to split the wood bases and breaking the hammers, I realized that attempting to make haste only impeded our progress. In that first week, we only covered sixty meters. At that rate, we wouldn't be finished until March! With six weeks left, we needed to average 157 meters a week. I wish we would have had time-lapse photography to highlight how this mission was accomplished. By doing so, one could see how one improves a routine by working together as a team and thinking through problems by taking the time to overcome obstacles and proceed without unnecessary haste.

Twenty-Four Hours in Phu Bai, Circa 1971

The routine in the fields of the Phu Bai ASP site set a positive cadence of field duty that was unfortunately set during the worst possible time of year in this region of central Vietnam. The rather critical mission was ill timed. In retrospect, this work should have been done from August through September. The monsoons in the second week were the worst of my entire field experience in Vietnam. Our detail continued operations every day, with ten hours a day of actual work in the field. The days were getting shorter due to the limited light at that time of year, along with the darkness caused by the heavy water-laden clouds. The troops progressed at a faster rate as the rhythm of teamwork started to take hold. My sergeant in charge was good at making sure the men were constantly moving forward. He even solved problems in the swamp area as we moved northward into the deepening water and aided in quick decisions as to what equipment and materials were needed in the deep-water areas.

By the second week, the routine started at 05:00 hours, with morning chow at 05:30, attendance at 06:15, and travel by trucks on the ASP road to the work site. The inventory of equipment and material would take place, and the teams would be on the construction site by 07:00 hours. At that time of year, along with the cloudy skies, the visibility in the morning was limited since there was also fog to contend with, not to mention the steady rainfall that didn't abate during the day. The working conditions meant that all concerned were soaking wet throughout the day. There was no dry area for the troops to chow down, and Stickney and I made the decision that the guys needed hot food. Although it cost us valuable time, we trucked the troops back to the mess hall each afternoon for a quick hot meal. This cost us an hour and a half a day, but in the end, the old saying that an army marches on its stomach would pay dividends in the accomplishment of our mission.

With the rain pelting our faces, the day would continue through the afternoon and into the murky dusk of evening. It was imperative that we cleared the ASP road by 18:30 hours each night as the reinforced infantry company security forces were setting up their claymore mines and setting their fields of fire. The days were long, but the on-site time was only ten hours. We had to work smart and limit our mistakes and solve obstacle problems as they occurred. Duties had to be delegated, and you had to trust the judgment of the people working for you. As soon as we moved off-site, we headed for the mess hall. Once fed, everyone headed to his assigned hooch. The EM (enlisted men) were housed in four-man sandbagged huts.

The officers had a larger sandbagged building with a common room and individual rooms. There were no plumbing facilities. To shave, one used cold water and a container; showers were in a separate outside facility using rainwater, which we had plenty of. Even in the humid and acrid air of Phu Bai, the art of taking a shower was a quick operation, as the shower was no more than a room constructed of plywood with a showerhead. The water emanated from a top-feeding water bucket that was collecting the monsoon rainwater. The showers were cold and exhilarating; one always moved quickly in taking a shower. We would head out to the shower nightly, getting soaking wet on the way. After showering, we would not wipe down but would just trudge back to the hooch, where we would dry ourselves with OD (olive drab) towels once we were inside. We had a generator providing electric power for light, but any windows were blacked out at night. Since we had no plumbing, we used a three-seat outhouse. Ah, all the comforts of home. We were lucky with a three-seater; the EM had ever-stinking eight-seater outhouses for every two hooches.

It was important to change daily since our clothing became soaked during the day, and we also rotated dry boots for the wet ones. The boots would begin to rot after one full week, and the green canvas uppers would gradually turn brown. As was common throughout Vietnam, we utilized hooch maids to clean our uniforms and to put a daily coat of polish on the lower part of the boots to try to repel water, which in reality was a waste of time. In the seven weeks in the fields of Phu Bai, I must have gone through ten pairs of boots. The hooch maid assigned to our billet was from nearby Hue. She was a widow who had lost her husband and child in the Tet Offensive of 1968. Her vocabulary was a mix of Vietnamese, French, and Pidgin English. Most of the maintenance officers assigned to our billet treated her as if she were nothing but a slave and had no respect for her well-being or dignity. I found this treatment reprehensible and on occasion made my thoughts known as to their mistreatment. Her main concern was that she would lose her job since many of the troops in Phu Bai would pull out with the completion of the ASP fortifications.

Usually at night, Stickney and I would go through our progress of the site construction for the day and plan on the logistics and obstacles facing us the next day. In Vietnam, the outgoing artillery started at 20:00 hours, and though just down the road, the earth trembled, and the cadence began as the battery sent out fire missions and H&I fire all night long. The sounds of the night in Vietnam were vivid; the rain was pelting down in droves, the mess hall had AFVN (Armed Forces

149

Vietnam Network) blasting from the cook's kitchen, and the artillery was firing off its version of pain for "Victor Charlie" (the VC). As Ralphie would say in *A Christmas Story* as he fell asleep with his Red Ryder BB gun, "All is right with the world!" Now, mind you, this daily routine was a full seven-days-a-week cycle; there were no days off in a combat zone. In fact, in their one-year tour of Vietnam, all personnel received only five days off for an out-of-country R & R (rest and recuperation).

Life in Phu Bai was exhausting and not unlike the feeling a marathon runner has when he only wants to reach the finish line. If I were a painter, I would look at my palette and mix black and white to form the color gray. When I think of Phu Bai in the realm of color, it was gray. Another analogy would be to film everything in black and white. Believe me, Phu Bai was not in Technicolor! The picture of the fields showed a drab grayness of daytime, and was grayer still heading into the dusk of the evening. This painted a vivid scene of Phu Bai as the artillery in the background served as a symphony to the ears of the soldier drifting off to sleep. To add to the grayness, the next day the drudgery would repeat the cycle all over again. It was like the movie *Groundhog Day*, recycling the same routine with only slight variations. Each trooper dreamed of freedom, which was but a mere dream at that time.

Troopers in the Field—Who Were They?

Frankly, it has taken me over forty years to come to terms with the men who I was in command of when accomplishing the mission. As Toto writes, men in Vietnam were using drugs. Bob was more versed in identifying personnel using opium and heroin than I was. My men did not use drugs; if they did, I never detected such use. My major problem was that they were smart and chose their high with the cheap offerings of liquor offered by the PX system, whiling away their evening hours with top-shelf alcoholic beverages. When gathering in the morning formations before heading out to the ASP, I encountered many instances in which I had to coax a reluctant trooper to head out onto the fields of Phu Bai.

The highest grade NCO was an E-5 (buck sergeant) who was a

quartermaster sergeant with an immense personality. His personality was tailored to our mission at hand. He had the ability to lead and guide the rest of the enlisted men to accomplish the tasks at hand. His demeanor was that of a conniving wheeler and dealer who dealt in gaining whatever advantage he could obtain. The other twenty-four men followed his counsel and leadership without any doubt. It was my responsibility to channel his leadership abilities to obtain the ultimate direction of my mission and to complete the ASP fortification as quickly as possible. It was my duty to direct and guide this young NCO in helping me complete my ultimate mission. The all-relevant question was how was I to convince this young NCO to acquiesce to my detailed plan?

After the disastrous first week, this group started to work together, and they were proceeding at a pace that would have allowed us to meet our deadline if we would have started from square one with such a demeanor. Somehow I had to make this group move about 20 percent faster, but how? I talked to Stickney about how we could incentivize these guys, but in Vietnam, what carrots can be dangled to entice twenty-five men who were "short" (not much time left in the Vietnam tour) to trudge along with a bit more alacrity? Stickney, being the "Ivy League Yalie" that he was, came up with a brilliant idea. "Why don't we guarantee a one-week in-country R & R at China Beach in Da Nang?" Great idea, but we needed to set a target date before Christmas Day of 1971, and we needed command approval. The next morning, I was off to see Lieutenant Colonel F, seeking his approval for all EM to be given one week of in-country R & R if the target date was met before Christmas Day. He gladly agreed, stating that it was a brilliant idea and to inform the men as soon as possible.

I immediately saddled up in my jeep and headed out to the site, signaling the good sergeant for a conference. I told him to tell the men that *he* arranged for in-country R & R upon the completion of our mission before Christmas. I wanted him to get the credit so he would have complete control and trust as a fellow EM, not that of an officer.

From that point on, there seemed to be a new attitude and purpose in the efforts of all the teams. Battling through the weather, with the blistered hands and jungle rot forming on their feet due to being constantly in the water, they were moving at a faster clip. The days melded into one another. Remember, there was no rest, only the incessant thumping of outgoing ordnance each night, with the rain battering up against the sandbagged hooches and the faraway echoes of AFVN refraining every hour "From the Mekong Delta to the DMZ, you're listening to AFVN. The time is 01:00 hours. Good morning, Vietnam."

Pinocchio Would Have Been Proud!

Regardless of what responsibilities or pressures I had in the wonderful resort of Phu Bai, lest we forgot, I needed to write my letters of joy back to my family in "the world" (the United States). Below is an actual letter that I did indeed embellish, and as time wore on, the lies got bigger, to the point that Pinocchio would have been proud:

17 November 1971
Dear family,

> *Rest at ease— I'm alive and well in Phu Bai, South Vietnam! This is the garbage pit of the world! If you take a look at a map of Vietnam, I'm located about forty miles north of Da Nang. Well, it seems Nixon is telling the truth. It looks like all of the U.S. Army in Vietnam will be out of here by June. I'll be out of here in late April or early May.*
>
> *I went to San Francisco and had an orthopedist look at my ankle. I got a profile, which means I can't go in the field. My duties here will be mostly administrative, and I'll be working with a friend of mine who went through IOBC at Ft. Benning.*
>
> *Everything here is winding down. We're not losing any men at all, and we'll be pulling out of Phu Bai in January to go down to Da Nang. I hope everything's okay at home. In just five short months, I'll be home, no sweat.*
>
> *Please send me airmail envelopes. We can't even steal any here. Also, send me some Dial shampoo. We can't get any shampoo here. Also, Mom, if you could send some fudge, I'd*

*really like it. It seems like the packages get over here quickly
and undamaged. So take it easy and God bless.*

*Love,
Dick*

*P.S. Dad, I made my first check out for $50 on November 6,
and my balance is $1041.75.*

Looking at these letters, it is evident that I was (and still am) a lousy liar. Pinocchio gave it away with his nose; I gave it away by putting it on too thick. Mom knew the truth; mothers can't be fooled!

This Isn't Norman Rockwell's Thanksgiving

It was Thursday, November 28, 1971, and to most GIs in the RVN, it was a normal day in a combat zone. The beat went on, the rain was pelting us in the field, the choppers continually hovered above, and we heard the sounds of guns being fired from the surrounding firebases in and along the A Shau Valley.

It was a standard tradition of all military units, whether stateside or in a combat zone, that every mess hall tried to bring the traditional Thanksgiving meal to the troops. We were no different. I escorted my men back to the mess hall for the meal. This turned out to be no ordinary meal. Our mess sergeant outdid himself and turned the frozen turkeys into a traditional home-style Thanksgiving feast fit for a king. True, it took two hours out of the day, but as a leader, it got me more Brownie points and appreciation from the troops, and those two hours lost turned into days gained in achieving the objective. To me, the mission was the *raison d'être*. I was totally committed to the task. I have to admit that even though I enjoyed the break from the routine and savored the delicious meal, I was still consumed with the mission and antsy to get back to work. The meal was only two short hours, but to the men it was like returning home for a brief time.

Dealing with an Unknown Enemy

Stickney and I walked through the torrential shower storms and entered the orderly room. We were clearly interrupting a rather serious discussion between Captain Farmer and the first sergeant. It seemed that the maintenance company was to supply a unit of graves registration and an EOD (explosives ordnance detachment) with vehicles to retrieve thirty-four bodies from a downed Chinook that had crashed. The chopper was not down due to hostile action; it crashed due to the weather conditions. The chopper was in the hills that ran parallel to the Hai Van Pass, and the EOD team was needed to clear the bodies of any booby traps that the VC (Vietcong) would put on the deceased to kill more GIs. The types of booby traps used would vary widely, sometimes using pressure release type mines or trip wire devices with C4 charges. Welcome to the Republic of Vietnam!

It was the Sunday after Thanksgiving, and after a long and grueling day, we headed for the mess and had our evening dinner. I have long forgotten what I ate, but as I analyze what happened some forty years ago, it had nothing to do with what I ate that evening. Stickney and I stuck to our normal routine of reviewing the day's activities and planning for the morrow. I felt weak and turned in relatively early, at about 21:00 hours, with a sour stomach, which I attributed to heartburn. The steady cadence of the outgoing artillery battery put me to sleep, and I drifted off in much need of a good night's rest. At 03:00 hours, I woke up with terrible chests pains. I started to throw up violently and was in total pain and disbelief as I struggled to get my bearings to the outhouse. It was raining buckets outside, the artillery was pounding out its cadence, and in the background, the mess hall radio was carrying a live NFL feed from Houston, Texas, with the Cleveland Browns playing the Houston Oilers. I was in pain as I carried my heaving and convulsing body toward the outhouse. As I stumbled through the heavy rains getting soaking wet, I entered the outhouse and dropped to my knees, continuing my heaving over the next fifteen minutes. The stench and circumstances I found myself in at that time will be firmly inscribed in my memory for the rest of my life.

It was truly surreal. Here I was, over ten thousand miles from home, throwing up in a godforsaken outhouse and listening to AFVN, with Gib Shanley, my hometown announcer, calling a game of my beloved Browns in Houston, Texas. It felt like a nightmare and made about as much sense. But what was happening to me was not a nightmare—where all I had to do was wake up! Not only was I throwing up, but I also had to use the seat because I had a severe case of diarrhea. I was in that outhouse until 04:30 hours. I stumbled back to the hooch and collapsed on my cot. I had a cold sweat and still had incredible chest pains, which if I didn't know any better, would have made me think I was having a heart attack. I lay on my cot until 05:00 hours, knowing my next move was to go on sick call and get this taken care of. When Stickney arrived at my room, he assisted me to sick call, and I sat in place for the next hour, waiting for the doctor to see me.

A rather young and overweight doctor examined me. He checked out my heart and said, "Lieutenant, you have nothing wrong with your heart, but you have severe acid indigestion." He gave me three bottles of Maalox along with the instructions to eat nothing solid for the next three days. He said to drink water and consume soup broth for sustenance and to prevent dehydration. The Maalox helped with the chest pains, but I still had diarrhea and was throwing up. God bless my mess sergeant, who specially made a vat of beef broth for me. The next three days, I was still making frequent visits to the outhouse, but as the days transpired, the less frequently I visited "my friend." By the fourth day, I was back in the field.

A Long-Overdue Diagnosis

Thirty-three years later, when visiting my doctor on Long Island, I related to him the story of the severe stomach problems I'd had in Vietnam. He told me that what I had experienced was common to many soldiers in Southeast Asia. A virus had probably entered my body in the water supply. He had a rather long and medically technical term for this disease, which has escaped me. In summary, I lost ten pounds in a period of one week. Even though I returned to my field duties after four days, I was without solid food for over a week. The only good things about being in the horizontal position for several days were that my ankle was no longer swollen and my feet actually dried out.

Going Solo

The days rambled on. The artillery fired off its missions each night, the rain continued its beating serenade against the sandbagged hooches, and the mess continued to play AFVN, which told us each and every hour "From the Mekong Delta to the DMZ, you're listening to AFVN." As one looked down from the first tier road of the ASP, the fortifications were steadily moving from right to left, from south to north, from servitude to freedom and mission accomplished. It was the first week of December, and we were proceeding on schedule.

At this time, the army, in its infinite wisdom, called upon the talents of Lieutenant Thomas Stickney. He received orders to become the property book officer (PBO) of the maintenance company. The company lacked a CWO (chief warrant officer) and was in need of a responsible officer to help in standing down the assets of the unit, which was in the process of returning to the continental United States. Their choice was correct, but in all selfishness, how was I supposed to operate? In essence, I was the motivational officer who was to inspire and lead the troops to bigger and better things; Tom quietly took care of all those "administrative details." In the good old army parlance, I was to suck it up and take on those extra duties. I did, and I actually survived as my E-5 continued to lead the troops through the thick swamp and move on to more shallow waters. We proceeded at a clip of two hundred meters a week.

In the meantime, Stickney needed another officer to accompany him to Long Binh with property book in hand to get his final instructions. To this day, I have no idea why I had to go with Tom on this on this trip to Long Binh. This incursion was to encompass two days, which was time away from the mission. The night before I left with Tom, I held a conference in the mess hall with my E-5 to strategize the next two days of operations. I had astutely stockpiled all the necessary equipment needed for the fortifications, including the much-needed sledgehammers and extra gloves and boots. I told him that it was imperative to cover at least forty meters in the next two days. He actually did better than that and went sixty meters. When I returned from Long Binh, I knew in my heart that our mission would be accomplished a full week before the deadline.

My only problem was making sure our fortifications were up to specifications, and I drilled into my sergeant that quality was more important than proceeding with substandard construction. On several instances, I would have sections torn down and rebuilt. In the ensuing time, my NCO did the same, and it made the troopers think that their leaders did care. Even though Stickney was no longer among us, his presence was felt as we strived to complete the task.

The Oasis of Long Binh

Tom and I had been in the monsoons of Phu Bai for little more than a month, and we hadn't really seen the light of day or the semblance of anything like the sun. We boarded a C-130 with the rain pelting the plane, and in very little time, we landed at Long Binh. As we exited the plane, the sun was blinding to our eyes. If Phu Bai was a palette of gray, then Long Binh possessed a full array of brilliant colors. While black-and-white film represented Phu Bai, Technicolor was the film of choice in Long Binh. The whole scene was quite the cultural shock to Tom and me.

We were met by a spec 5 (E-5 specialist) dressed in Class A TWs (dress tropical worsted uniform). He drove us to US Army Command Vietnam. As we entered the gates of the complex, we noted that there were no temporary buildings made of plywood, and that all personnel were in dress uniforms with their ribbons and spit-shined boots. Stickney and I were in rumpled and faded jungle fatigues with well-worn boots that were turning brown from their original green canvas tops and black polished bottoms. We must have looked a sight! We entered the headquarters of Army Command Vietnam and were amazed to find marble floors and well-lit hallways with military memorabilia tastefully displayed. We made our way to a posh room where we would conference with the powers-to-be and receive detailed instructions for Lieutenant Stickney to proceed in the standing down of all the equipment of the assets of the property book.

I was told that I was only a "security escort" to assist Lieutenant Stickney, as required by army regulation. I wasn't going to argue, since in my short tour of Vietnam, I never had an R & R, and this two-day trip would suffice as time off from my duties in the field. Hell, I'd take what I could get; when in Vietnam, one was always looking for an "easy day."

Tom and I were dumbfounded by the facilities. These "Saigon warriors" had hot and cold running water. They had ice-cold water coolers. The enlisted barracks were made of concrete block and were air-conditioned. Everyone was wearing clean uniforms, and they had females all over the place. These females had round eyes; they were American civilian workers in dresses. Stickney and I thought that we had died and gone to heaven. My God, those people had no idea that there was a war going on. It seemed so strange to me that these army personnel were drawing the same combat pay that I was drawing. It didn't seem right forty-one years ago, and it still doesn't seem right now, but it was a fact: they were in a different world than we were dealing with in the fields of Vietnam. While there, we ate in a swank officers' mess and actually took in a movie in a real theater. It was a tough job, but someone had to do it. The next morning, reality set in, and off we went, from Long Binh to the wonderful auspices of Phu Bai.

I vividly remember traveling back along the roads of Long Binh and seeing these beautiful Eurasian women (a mixture of French and Vietnamese) riding on their mopeds in their *ao dais*. As I carefully looked around the buildings in this Saigon suburb, I noticed the French influence of architecture in all the surroundings. What I remember is a strange and exotic mixture of Europe and Asia, combined in a colonial setting soon to be lost to all. As we landed in Phu Bai, I saw nothing exotic or enticing. My in-country R & R abruptly ended.

Explaining the Definition of a Lawful Order to a Superior

I returned to my duties in the field sans Stickney. I felt naked! As I reached the ASP site, I was surprised to see the progress made. We were over halfway to completion, and as I perused the lay of the land, I saw that the swamp in the northern sector was much less swampy. I turned to my trusty sergeant and said, "If we continue this way, we'll be finished by the seventeenth. How about it, Sarge?"

The only thing he said was, "Sir, do they have girls with bikinis at China Beach?"

I looked him straight in the eye and said, "Hell, Sarge, I don't know. There's only one way of finding out!"

After our lively exchange, I went over to take inventory of our supplies and equipment. Damn, we were running low on everything. I sloshed my way back to the field, where the good sergeant was supervising the troops, and told him to hold down the fort, as I had to go back to the orderly room to secure requisitions for supplies, and then I had to take the trek to Camp Eagle to secure our order.

As I was sloshing back to the truck, out of the corner of my eye, to my immediate right, I saw a captain, and he was calling out to me: "Lieutenant, I need your help."

As I approached, I said, "Sir, what's the problem?"

"You see that deuce and a half with your driver in it? I need it right now!"

My immediate thoughts: *Who the hell is this guy? Does he have any concept of what I am doing here?* I looked him straight in the eye, with the rain drenching both of us, and said, "Excuse me, sir. That's my driver and my truck, and come hell or high water, you can't use those assets!"

"Well, Lieutenant, I'm a captain, and if I order you to give me that truck and driver, you have no recourse!"

"Let me get this straight," I said. "You're ordering me to give you my truck and driver?"

"That's correct, Lieutenant. You're in the army now!"

"Sir, do you have any concept of what is a legal order and what is not? I'll answer that for you—you have no clue! Now listen to me closely; I'll relinquish these assets only under the command of Lieutenant Colonel F. I'm on a highly critical mission, and you, sir, are pissing on my parade!"

"You can't talk to me like that, Lieutenant. I'll have you court-martialed!"

In return, I said, "Your nonsense is no concern of mine. If you have any complaints or questions, go see my boss, Lieutenant Colonel F. Otherwise, get the hell out of my way; I've got a job to do!"

At that point in my military career, I couldn't care less about the intentions of a wayward captain looking for a driver and truck. To this day, I have no clue as to what he was doing or where he was going. For all I knew, he could have been the opposite of Clarence the good angel in *It's a Wonderful Life*. Instead, this captain was from *Bizzaro World*; he was the evil demon intended to foil all my good-intentioned plans. He appeared in my life, gave me instant and real grief, and then exited my life as I stood my ground. Hell, I essentially felt like Gary Cooper in the 1952 movie *High Noon*. I stuck to my guns, and the evil bastard trying to cause me grief was gunned down! Orders are orders; make sure the person giving them has the proper authority to execute them. I guess I won this battle at the OK Corral.

Camp Eagle—What to Do with an ARVN Captain?

My day had already started with an eccentric captain. What would transpire along the route to Camp Eagle? I entered the headquarters of the 101st Airborne Division in search of division G-4 (division supply) to secure the necessary supplies for the completion of my "critical" mission. I entered the sacred grounds of Division G-4 and met a rather senior E-8 (master sergeant) who inspected my requisitions and immediately had a crew of six men loading my truck. In no longer than sixty minutes, I was headed out of Camp Eagle and down the road to perdition.

My driver was a spec 5 (specialist fifth class), a good old southern boy who was an enlistee and not a drafted EM. He was from Alabama, and in today's context of political persuasion, he would be a right-wing Tea Party advocate. He made no qualms as to what he believed in or what his political persuasions were. I liked this rather gruff redneck. He was concise in his habits and ever faithful to my commands. The rain was falling at the usual monsoon rate as we traveled back to Phu Bai.

In the distance, I noticed the form of a human body waving frantically to us. As we got closer to the person, I noticed that he was an ARVN (Army of the Republic of Vietnam) captain trying to stop us. I turned to my driver and told him to stop. He immediately said, "Sir, make sure to have your hand on your forty-five. I don't trust him." I answered in the affirmative and got out of the truck. In broken English, the ARVN captain walked to the back of the truck and asked if I wanted to sell him the contents. He went to his pocket and pulled out a wad of twenty-dollar bills that were not MPC but actual greenbacks. I hadn't seen real greenbacks since I'd left the Ninety-Second Replacement Battalion in Long Binh. Obviously, this good captain was dealing in the black market. Not only was he dealing for personal profit, he was probably aiding the cause of the VC infrastructure in the area. I immediately told him to *didi mou* (Vietnamese for "go away"), but he persisted by waving more money in my face. I didn't waste any time, and I made the motion to un-holster my sidearm. The captain immediately put his arms up, and I continued telling him to *didi mou* as he was literally running down the road in the direction of Camp Eagle.

I know it's over forty years later, but a question just occurred to me: He was on foot with no form of transportation in sight—how did he get there, and where in the hell was he running to? My driver was shouting at me to shoot him, but I had no intention of doing that. In retrospect, the son of a bitch was probably a VC impersonating an ARVN captain or was a corrupt ARVN soldier. It was at that moment that I was convinced that once we pulled out of Vietnam, the North Vietnamese would win the war. The government and its own military, which were supposed to be our allies, were nothing but a corrupt regime trying to live off the aid that we, their defenders, were providing. From that point on, I wanted nothing to do with a government so blatantly corrupt, and our command most certainly knew what was transpiring around them. Somehow we made it back to the ASP before dark, where we unloaded all the necessary supplies and equipment.

Going into the Stretch

As my detachment was heading back to base that eventful day, I realized that with the progress we were making, we would be done within two weeks. That night, as in most nights in Phu Bai, it was raining in torrents, the guns were blasting their cadence, and AFVN was playing the current top forty for all to hear: "From the Mekong Delta to the DMZ ..." I didn't tell a soul about my adventures in the field. Up until now, only my driver and I knew the full story of what had happened.

As I drifted off to a fitful sleep, my only negative thoughts were that upon the ARVN inspection of our fortifications, they would not sign off on acceptance. The next morning, I took my sergeant with me to the ASP site. We walked all the way to the south side, adjacent to the French minefield. This was our original starting point. He and I did a thorough walk around with "inspection eyes" to verify the integrity of our work. I was straining to find the slightest thing wrong. Neither of us found any problems with the construction at the site.

Even though we were still experiencing torrential rains, I started to notice that in the late morning, we would have a slick (UH helicopter) constantly circling the ASP. Later, when I was performing staff work in Da Nang, I found out that General Sweeney and his chief of staff were measuring our progress every day, such was the importance of this mission. Thank God I didn't know this at the time. It would have made me even more anxious than I already was. We continued going from right to left, south to north, and we were covering almost forty meters a day. The end was in actual sight, and as we got closer to our final objective, all could feel the movements and determination of the working teams. The fact that the EM were incentivized could be seen, and they were already dreaming of a bikini-laden beach of round-eyed females enticing them on China Beach.

We became so determined in our mission that we started moving too fast. While running through the swamp, a trooper fell on the pointed edge of an engineer stake and gashed a main artery in his leg. One of his team members used his jungle fatigue jacket as a tourniquet to stop the bleeding. The wound was rather severe, and we evacuated the trooper immediately, utilizing the deuce and a half to take him to the medical facilities. That soldier received his million-dollar wound, and since he was short, he headed for the final goal of boarding a freedom bird with a destination ticket punched for the world. This screwed up my team integrity. I added the members of the injured soldier's team to other teams as we motored on. Since we were moving at a fast clip, my duties as a purveyor of supplies and equipment increased, and I had to make frequent trips to Camp Eagle.

The Ugly Americans

About December 11, I had to trek to the orderly room to pick up the standard requisition forms I needed to secure the supplies and equipment needed for the mission. On this particular day, when I walked into the orderly room, I found a buck sergeant screaming at the compound "shit burner" (excrement waste person) about stealing items in the EM quarters. The sergeant was literally kicking this Vietnamese man and slapping him around in full sight of the first sergeant and myself. He claimed that this "papa-san" was absconding with the valuables of the resident EM. As the sergeant went on an absolute tirade and physically abused this Vietnamese man, I became uncomfortable with the whole situation. As the senior ranking person in that room, I knew I had to do something, but I had no idea if the Vietnamese man had stolen anything.

It didn't matter if he had stolen anything or not—what the sergeant was doing was wrong. Moreover, this scenario took place right in front of the first sergeant, who essentially knew better. Remarkably, the first sergeant (Top) did nothing. I firmly asked the sergeant to stop his antics. Rather startled, he looked up at me and said, "Sir, these bastards need to be taught a lesson!"

I looked him right in the eye and said, "Sergeant, this is an orderly room of the US Army. What you are doing is against regulation. It's time to take him outside and release him. He has killed no one, nor has he been proven to be a thief! Even if you confirm his theft, you can't treat him this way. Please cease and desist!"

The Vietnamese man was moved outside, and he left the base. In the meantime, I looked at the first sergeant and asked him why he hadn't objected. He told me this was his last tour of Vietnam, and that he didn't want to rock the boat. I was pissed and told him in no uncertain terms that as the first sergeant, it was his duty to maintain discipline and decorum. Top looked at me with a smirk and said,

"This is my last combat tour. I have two months left, and I don't need any complications, sir!"

I looked at him and said, "Top, if you're old and tired, you should have hung them up before this tour! You aren't doing your job!" I left the orderly room thoroughly pissed. I realized that our attitude toward the indigenous population was self-serving and gave no credence to the local culture. After all, we were Americans, and everyone had to acquiesce to our culture, mores, and way of life. It sounds pompous and selfish. Indeed, we were the "ugly Americans." Shame on us!

In the last week, our undermanned detachment covered more ground than in any other week. By December 16, we had our inspection conducted under light rain. The captain representing the ARVN brigade only had one complaint. The entrance point had no secured gate. I immediately pointed out to the captain that the specifications did not call for a secured entrance gate. My immediate commander was Major K, who only in the last week had taken over for Lieutenant Colonel F, and he stated to the ARVN captain that the gate would be installed by an engineer battalion within twenty-four hours. On this statement, the release was signed.

By December 17, the fortification was complete. The mission was accomplished! Stickney was still in the process of standing down the assets of the maintenance company. My orders were to report the Da Nang Support Command. On the evening of December 17, I heard the last of the steady cadence of artillery fire along with my constant companion of the mess hall, the AFVN. With the mission accomplished, I felt the satisfaction of completion such as I have never felt before or since. Nobody could or would take that away from me.

Outgoing

As night falls,
The rain continues,
The long day slumbers,
And the battery awakes
In all its blazing glory.
The Earth shakes,
A certain rhythm it takes.

A cadence takes hold,
The targets are unknown.
The projectiles are hopeful
Of finding the enemy unfold.
Only hear the pulsations
Of the battery awakened.
The cadence continues
On through the night.
As the soldier of the field
Sleeps on to morning bright.

Thoughts of the fields of Phu Bai, circa 1971
Richard C. Geschke

CHAPTER 17
VIETNAM ... MY GOD, THEY REALLY SENT ME THERE!

A Toto Chapter

I ask the reader's forgiveness for telling only some of the parts of my short journey in Vietnam. Some things are too painful to remember.

They want me to go where?

I came down on orders for Vietnam in the summer of 1971. I couldn't believe the phone call I received from the assistant S-1. "Bob, I have received some alert orders for you." He paused for what seemed like an eternity and said, "You're going to Vietnam."

It couldn't be happening to me. I'd just come back from a leave in Switzerland and Italy, and I was convinced that President Nixon's plan for Vietnamization was working. Why would they send me when units were being dismantled in Vietnam and were being returned to various points around the globe? Why would the Pentagon send to Vietnam a first lieutenant infantry who had never served in a line unit? It didn't make any sense.

My route to Vietnam was not a direct one. Geschke and I were sent to the subtropical paradise that was the Jungle Operations

Warfare School at Ft. Sherman, Panama. Once we finished with the delights of living with the "snake eaters," I flew to McCord AFB (air force base) for my flight to Vietnam. I remember boarding the plane, and honest to God, I thought that our plane would be rerouted. I had no such luck. We stopped in Fairbanks, Alaska, Yacoda AFB in Japan, and then Vietnam. I landed at Cam Ranh Bay Air Base at about 02:30 hours.

My God, I'm in Vietnam!

When the plane's tires hit the runway, I finally received my cold shower. I was in Vietnam. My first thoughts: *Those sons of bitches really sent me here.* Up to that exact moment, I thought that I would be spared this test. You knew that you had landed in a different place. As soon as the plane (Flying Tiger Airlines) was safely on the runway, all the lights were turned off so we wouldn't make a great target. Lord have mercy on me! Come to think of it, Flying Tiger Airlines was the only plane that did not have their initials on the tail stabilizer. I guess the army didn't want FTA (fuck the army) on display, especially on a "freedom bird," as it was called in Vietnam.

Welcome to Your New Home

So here I was, an FNG (fucking new guy) being introduced to the wonders of Vietnam. We were assigned temporary barracks and told to get some sleep. We awoke to the sound of an E-7 telling us that we had a briefing that morning at 08:00, officers and enlisted alike. Meanwhile, I had to go to the latrine to relieve myself, so I wandered into the nearest five-seater and started to do my business. Suddenly, a mama-san entered the latrine, with me half-naked and on the throne. She proceeded to take the seat next to mine, "dropped trou," and did her thing. Welcome to Vietnam!

Where Are They Sending Me?

Later that afternoon, we were issued jungle fatigues and jungle boots.

We also had to turn in all our greenbacks (dollars), exchanging them for MPCs (military payment certificates). It looked like Monopoly money. I remember that the twenty-dollar certificate had a picture of Sitting Bull on the front, and the ink color was purple. We could keep our "silver." This exchange of money was to prevent the black market from using our funds. MPCs were changed several times during the year to stop illegal transactions.

The next morning, officers were given a "dream sheet" on which to indicate their preference for assignment in Vietnam. The choices were mind-numbing: 1st Cav Division, 23rd Infantry Division and the 101st Airborne Division. Now, there were some "dream" choices, such as Saigon Support Command, Da Nang Support Command, and Cam Ranh Support Command. Well, I knew that if I chose one of the infantry divisions, I was sure to go there, so I put down Cam Ranh, Saigon, and Da Nang support commands. I would go down swinging for my choices. A captain next to me glanced at my choices and told me that I was nuts to make those choices. He urged me to choose one of the infantry divisions. I declined.

Later that day, I paid some Vietnamese stitchery a few MPCs to have my name and "US Army" with my crossed rifles embroidered on my uniform. I also had my cigarette lighter etched with a cartoon character. We waited for our assignments. Shortly afterward, we were told our assignments were posted outside the barracks. We all scrambled to the posting. I slowly read the names and found mine. I turned to the left to read what I was sure was bad news: TOTO, ROBERT A., CAM RANH SUPPORT COMMAND.

There Was Joy in Mudville!

I was overwhelmed with joy! The same captain who had encouraged me to select an infantry company was stunned. He wished me luck. I was contacted by a member of the Fifty-Second Transportation Command, and a jeep picked me up at about 10:30 hours. I reported to my new command and was asked to produce my personnel file. About thirty minutes later, a command sergeant major stood in front of me and asked, "Lieutenant, how the hell did you end up in the infantry? With your background, you should be in finance or AG (Adjutant General)."

I said, "Sergeant Major, I agree with your conclusions, but here we are. I would appreciate any assignment you have."

The Curse of the Crossed Rifles!

He then asked me if I wanted to work on the dock, supervising the unloading of ships in the bay. Well, I knew that North Vietnam did not have a navy, so I eagerly accepted the assignment. I met my future boss, a transportation captain, just before the lunch hour. He explained my future duties and invited me for lunch. We traveled by jeep to the officers' club. Then trouble struck. We were seated at a table with an ADA (Air Defense Artillery) captain, who was the CO of the only infantry company within fifty miles. He saw the crossed rifles on my lapel and spoke. "Why is command assigning you to the docks when I'm short an infantry lieutenant?" I felt a cold chill down my back. I finished lunch and headed back to the docks. Within the hour, I was reassigned to the Fifty-First Infantry Company. I was shell-shocked. I reported to the CO, and he spelled out my duties in about five minutes. He told me I would be accompanying another lieutenant that evening and would be leaving at about 17:00 hours. He said to leave my belongings with him. The lieutenant would fill me in on my regular duties.

I had chow and waited for 17:00 hours. I didn't know where we were going, what our mission was, how many men would be under my command, how many positions, what to do if attacked, what the rules for engagement were, and so on. We traveled to the checkpoint north of Cam Ranh. We had fixed position bunkers and a command bunker with telecommunications and listening equipment. The men were to take guard duty for two hours at a time, with two men per bunker. I was told to relax for a while.

My Introduction to a Line Unit

About 19:30 hours, it was plenty dark, and the other lieutenant told me that he was leaving for a few hours and would return. I never saw that idiot again. So I was in charge of X men, with X mission, without having any idea where I was. About midnight, I talked with my NCOs. I told them that I was relying on them to "nursemaid" me through the night because I had not been briefed. I told them that I knew they would do their jobs, and that the next time I was with them, I would be better prepared. Later on, an E-6 who was on duty that night told me that my admissions were well accepted by the NCOs, and that they felt I was going to be okay.

Our main mission, as I later learned, was to staff positions at the checkpoint, which was a bridge over Cam Ranh Bay. We would have positions over and under the bridge, along with the defense of Cam Ranh Airport. We also had bunkers up and down the coast as far as Phan Rang, where we had another platoon of soldiers. These bunkers ran about thirty miles down the coast.

The coastal bunkers were only staffed at night or when we had heightened levels of security. The checkpoint bridge and airport positions were staffed during the day. Under the bridge, we had seven catwalks, where the soldiers' duties were to look for enemy frogmen. We had radiotelephone devices, rifles, illumination flares, and spotlight nightscopes. We had moving guard posts on both sides of the bridge. We were constantly subjected to 90mm rocket attacks. The enemy's main objective was trying to hit the bridge, the airport, and any surrounding personnel. Hitting us would be a bonus.

Moon Phases and Learning the Routine

We worked seven days a week, always at night. I learned to love the phases of the moon. I read the daily intelligence report and recorded the challenge and password protocol. Also I studied illumination data on the moon. But from new moon to about 17-percent full, I was very much on guard. The routine almost never changed. I was always tired. I was getting about four hours of sleep, if I was lucky. I slept from 09:15 to about 13:30 hours. Trying to fall asleep in the heat was difficult, even though I was tired.

Oh, about that lieutenant who was supposed to have trained me on my duties … I heard that he traveled back to base camp, about thirty miles south, and was involved in an accident. He had dressed up in a sergeant's uniform, gotten drunk with an NCO buddy, and rolled a jeep. He and his friend ended up in a hospital. The lieutenant was charged with DUI, conduct unbecoming an officer, and impersonating an NCO. I think he was dishonorably discharged from the service.

About three weeks after my indoctrination, the command staff discovered that I had not attended a two-day mandatory training session on drugs. This class would later prove to be useful. I learned about marijuana, heroin, and all sorts of pills (four-way tabs, uppers, downers, and so on). I learned that heroin distributed in Vietnam was so powerful that it caused serious body injury, like strokes and massive constipation. Some soldiers had taken enough heroin that their waste had become solidified like cement and had to be surgically removed. We are talking about nineteen-year-old kids. What a tragedy!

My duties became routine. We had the security of the previously mentioned positions and were forced to deal with a lack of critical supplies, low morale, drugs, the weather, and did I forget to mention the enemy? The rules of engagement were very political. We were instructed to yell "*Dung lai!*" (Halt!) when we suspected an enemy agent, unless our "lives were in immediate danger." What a bunch of bull! We were not supposed to have any rounds chambered in our weapons, which was more a safety issue than anything else.

Watching for Charlie!

We had sampans heading toward the bay at all times during the day and night. We could not fire upon the sampans unless fired upon, even though they were in restricted waters. It was truly frustrating. One night, we encountered several sampans heading toward the bridge and the airport. My men were agitated that the sampans were allowed to be in the area, and that we couldn't fire upon them. Recall that we had illumination flares. I thought to myself, *What if I discharge an illumination flare parallel to the ground?* Well, my sick idea worked.

The flares followed the slope of the terrain, imploding near the heads of the sampan operators. They *didi mou*-ed (left in a hurry away from us) and retreated from the bay. We had achieved a victory of sorts, and we settled in for the moment. Remember that I was only a few years older than the majority of my enlisted men. We celebrated our victory with a chorus of applause; high fives had not yet been contemplated.

Locating Geschke and Maintaining Contact with the World

Wait a minute! I forgot to mention Geschke. I did not know where Dick was, and I wrote to his parents in Cleveland. I enclosed a letter to Dick in my correspondence. My letter reached Dick some twelve days later. At last, I knew where my buddy was stationed. Sometime later, we would talk in person.

Letters—oh my God, did I get letters. My brother had decided to place my name in a local newspaper in a "write-to-a-soldier" exercise. I was inundated with letters from a fourth-grade class in Lawrence, Massachusetts. I didn't want to disappoint these children, but where the hell was I going to find cards to send them a response? Shortly afterward, I was able to acquire a box of thank-you notes and send them to the children. I still have a soft spot in my heart for those kids. One kid used to send me cartoons and short jokes from *Reader's Digest*. She related stories in her letters that I'm sure her parents would have disapproved of. At least the postage was "free" as all outgoing mail sent by GIs in Vietnam didn't have to pay for stamps.

On my return trip to the United States, we again stopped in Japan. I bought a kimono and another trinket as a gift to the fourth grader. When I returned home, I called the home of the little girl and told her parents of my gift. I also said that if they did not approve of my bringing the gift by, then I could mail it. The mother of the girl said, "She's only eleven years old, you know." I said that I knew the girl's age and just wanted to give her a small gift. The mother finally relented, and I delivered the gift. Some ten years later, when my mother was checking into a hospital, the admission person asked her if she had a son named Robert. My mother answered yes, and the girl, who was then twenty-one years old, recounted the story. (Unfortunately, that is the way many returning Vietnam vets were treated. Many people's conception of returning vets were that they were all drug heads, murderers, and were not to be trusted. Thank God the treatment of veterans is better today).

Drugs

It is a travesty to say that everyone in Vietnam took drugs. It is just not true. Availability of drugs was something else. There was marijuana (Mary Jane), heroin (scag/horse), morphine, LSD, strychnine, hashish, and a myriad of uppers and downers. A "four-way" tab was one part LSD, one part morphine, one part strychnine, and one part downer. This was serious stuff. I had let my men know that taking drugs was not something I would tolerate. I would bust their bottoms if I caught them high.

Dealing with the "Enemy Within"

We shipped home one soldier who was paralyzed from the waist down because of heavy heroin use. The same soldier had been sent to detoxification several times, but it had not cured him of his addiction. One night while on guard duty, the same individual assaulted one of my sergeants. The sergeant was bloodied and angry. He was also at least fifteen years older than the soldier was. I asked the sergeant if he wanted to press charges, and he said no. All he wanted was for the soldier to be relieved. That was my job.

I approached the soldier, who was obviously high on drugs. He turned toward me and pointed his M-16 at me. We were only four feet apart. He said, "What do you want?"

I had to think of something quick or I was a goner. I said, "I understand that you are not feeling too well, and I was thinking of sending you back to base camp."

"You are not taking my weapon from me! Am I under arrest?"

I said, "Have I read you your rights? I could never place you under arrest without warning you of your rights, agreed?"

"Yeah, I guess so, but no tricks." I assured him that he was being sent back to base camp because of his health. He lowered his weapon, and we sent him back to base camp. I finally was able to exhale, and

I checked my underwear for stains. The E-6 was also sent back to receive medical attention, but in different vehicles.

After one of the shakedown inspections, several of my men turned up positive for drugs from the urinalysis testing. They agreed to enter the drug rehabilitation program with the understanding that their records would be expunged if they completed it. I had the next day off, my first day off in sixty days, and guess where I spent it. I was with these six juveniles in "rehab." I brought cigarettes, toothpaste, shaving cream, and books. These six were not "heads," and I couldn't understand why they had tested positive. Turns out, they had smoked an OJ, and the opiates showed up in the test. I persuaded five out of the six to complete the program, but my pleas fell upon deaf ears to one nineteen-year-old. He escaped the next night and was sent to the stockade the following week.

We had other soldiers who tried to get off drugs with the help of their buddies. Obviously these buddies were not addicted. Once I found out what was going on, I did my best to help these soldiers overcome their addiction by lightening their regular duties. Sometimes it worked; other times, I drew the short straw. I often wondered what happened to these young men. But they made their choices and were left to pay for their decisions.

Occasionally, we would receive a "congressional inquiry" about one of the members of the unit. Although the letter was usually signed by some high-ranking officer, the inquiry and letter were usually done and written by a company-level officer. Guess who usually got the job in my company? I was emotional when I had to write a parent that his son had been admitted to a drug detoxification center. The drug conflict in Vietnam would continue until the conflict was over. For many of these men, the struggle would continue back in the States.

Alcohol

What can I say about the "juicer"? Beer was the beverage of choice for the juicers. Beer was cool, greatly available, and cheap, and it was readily deposited into a "piss pipe." A piss pipe was a length of four-foot PVC pipe anchored into the ground at a forty-five-degree angle, and it was four feet in length. It was surrounded by four sheets of four-by-eight plywood with a walk-in entrance. There was some crushed rock at the base of the pipe and a screen mesh covering over the mouth of the pipe. These enclosures were strategically placed near common areas.

Since everyone was taller than four feet, it didn't take any imagination to tell what the personnel were doing while standing in the middle of the enclosure. After a while, you didn't even notice the person. All you knew was that you were next in line.

Beer was cheap in the military, hence its popularity among the troops. Everyone was looking to escape from the tedium and complexity of duty. Alcohol was more readily accepted by the majority of the servicemen. Those with not too much longevity didn't see the difference between drugs and alcohol—anything to escape from reality for some time. The implement of escape didn't really matter.

The situation changed daily, and as officers, we were expected to adapt. So much for the early days.

The Seasoning of Toto

I quickly learned that human relations skills were much more important than "combat" skills, at least as a first lieutenant. Here were young men, mostly nineteen- and twenty-year-olds, who were away from home and filled with unanswered questions. They wanted to be treated with respect and dignity and had to be able to believe in their leaders. I tried to be all those things and maybe more. They could only be convinced by actions and not false promises. They were truly remarkable.

In the military, there are numerous times for learning about the makeup of these young men. You can't believe how close you can get to an individual in such a short amount of time. Their most private thoughts are shared with their comrades; hopes, dreams, conflicts, home life, loves, and passions are all fair game. These young men exposed their very souls to the ears of their comrade. Everything was shared. If you ran out of cigarettes or food, your comrades were there. If you needed moral support, it was readily given. They were in this thing together. Even racial divides were overcome. These "grunts" were in the slop together.

I cannot adequately describe the concept of trust among soldiers. Sure, there were moments when your comrade screwed up, but those times were the exception. You had someone's back, and someone had yours. You depended upon your fellow soldier. The NCOs and officers were there to lead their troops. The troops depended upon them, and vice versa. It was a family—not necessarily a happy one but a family nonetheless.

Robert Toto taking in refreshment
December 25, 1971, during the Bob Hope Show in Long Binh

Happy New Year!

Amusing incidents did occur in Vietnam. I'll never forget one incident that happened on New Year's Eve. I just knew that the troops would be doing something silly on New Year's Eve, like setting off flares. So I personally went to each soldier at the checkpoint and told him that he could fire a flare at midnight, but he could not fire a red-star cluster, because that was the signal for pullback from the checkpoint. I had forgotten about the MPs. At one minute to midnight, flares and smoke of all colors and shapes lit up the sky. Then someone sent up a red-star cluster. I was absolutely livid. I started giving commands to the bunkers to remain in their positions. Then I went to find out who shot the red-star cluster.

I found the MP who had set off the flare, and I tore into him. I am not that tall, but that night I was ready to slam-dunk one MP. I asked him to repeat the plan for pullback to the checkpoint. He said that he didn't know it. Then I asked him the name of his platoon leader. Afterward, I instructed him on the pullback plan. He apologized. I told him that apologies were not necessary, but that he had better be familiar with the mission plan, or I would have a talk with his platoon leader. The message did not have to be repeated.

I forgot to mention that that same night, a full colonel showed up at the checkpoint with a female captain and a case of beer. He asked me to call in the men from their positions so a woman could greet them for New Year's and they could each have a can of beer. I thanked the colonel but declined the beer offer because we had well in excess of twenty-four men in the bunkers. I also said that it might be dangerous to bring the men up from the catwalks in the dark. He said it was New Year's and to lighten up. So I accompanied them to three foxholes, when suddenly small-arms fire broke out. I told them to run to the command bunker. It was a cold shower for both of them. Eventually, the small-arms fire subsided, and the "guests" were escorted from the area. "The road to hell is paved with good intentions."

About two weeks before I arrived in Vietnam, a contingent of men from my company was guarding the top catwalks of Cam Ranh Bridge. One soldier, walking the top of the bridge, stopped to position the spotlight, which was pointed toward the water. The soldier was high on drugs. Below him, he saw the shadow of a diver in the water. "Hey, man," he yelled, "what are doing down there?" He repeated this twice, until a soldier on one of the catwalks shouted, "Little, who are you talking to?" Little said, "That dude down there. He shouldn't be swimming there."

Suddenly, the soldier realized what was happening. He dropped a concussion grenade into the water, and an enemy frogman surfaced, bleeding from the ears. He was carrying explosives to blow up the bridge. The high soldier was still trying to talk with the frogman, unaware of what had really transpired.

There was always gambling. These guys would bet on anything—insects, shooting stars, when the next round would hit … I had some troops that absolutely begged me to play craps with them. I figured that it was worth the loss of a dollar, so I agreed. The first roll was a seven. I relinquished my dollar and told the specialist that I was through. He said, "L-T (meaning lieutenant and pronounced El Tee), you have to play again to get your money back." I said, "That dollar was my investment in you to stop pestering me. It was worth a buck."

The Shit-Burners of Vietnam

And then there were the "shit-burners." When the staff could not do anything with a trooper, the last resort was to make him a shit burner. These guys cleaned out the latrines, disinfected the area, and took turns burning the defecation. Fifty-five-gallon oil drums, cut in half, were filled with a combustible liquid, usually gasoline, and set afire. A great story for when a son asks, "Daddy, what did you do in the war?" In one of the other units, a guy had his life spared when he jumped into a fifty-five-gallon drum, being used for urination, when a grenade was thrown nearby. One of the other guys was not so lucky.

Again, I apologize to the reader for not relating other war stories. Sure, we had "fragging" incidents; sure, we had some acts of bravery, of fear, or the little parts of a conflict that make up the whole. I can tell you that I was so scared the first time I had to crawl out of my foxhole under rocket attack that I didn't know how I would react. Something moved me to action, however. I don't know the source of this strength, nor do I wish to relive that moment in writings. Some stories will not be told, but at the end of this chapter, I have included a poem I wrote that may help the reader to understand.

I heard through the grapevine that certain vol indefs who had been accepted to college were being given an early release. Well, I had been accepted to graduate school and was eager to explore the possibilities. After three weeks of misinformation, I found out that I was qualified for early release. I quickly gathered my wits and headed to the replacement company with my paperwork. I had waited several hours to phone my parents and give them the news. Then there was Geschke.

Breaking the News

I figured out how to call Dick in country, as I had done once before. When I got to the replacement company, I was extremely happy, but not happy that my friend would still be there. I reached him by phone. When I told him where I was, he said, "Toto, you're not leaving here, are you?" I had a tear in my eye when I told him I was going home. It was truly devastating. I promised to write.

A men's room in the replacement company had a chalkboard on the wall. You were encouraged to write comments on the board. Now bear in mind that the army tour in Vietnam was one year, 365 days. I was on my way to the men's room when I heard a series of laughs. I figured someone had written something funny. As I entered the latrine, I glanced up to the board. Someone had written 364 DAYS LEFT—SEEMS LIKE I FUCKIN' GOT HERE ONLY YESTERDAY!!!!! I did laugh but was still overcome with grief that I had to leave my buddy Dick.

After a short urinalysis test, the "freedom bird" was the next step. They told us we would be taking the southern route, which would have brought us to California as our final stop. The plane took off, and almost on cue, once we reached cruising altitude, everyone on the plane started applauding. I fell asleep. I awoke when the plane started to descend for our first stop. I looked out the window and saw Mount Fuji. What the hell? We were taking the northern route. We were rerouted. A final jab by the army.

Foxholes

Surrounded by sentinels of shadows and shapes-
your task to test nighttime nuances of nerves and natural
movements,
while serving those whose moments of rest comes not too often-
trusting that tired eyes and emaciated nerves remember the
training.
And the tricks
And the consequences of error.

179

Richard C. Geschke and Robert A. Toto

The night is seared by the concussion of pulsating pockets of
atmosphere.
Like expectant couples rehearsing the sounds of breathing,
the signature of incoming projectiles corrupts the bodily
functions
in a manner not meant to be natural.
And the impending ignition
And the daunting detonation.
Animal instincts fly against the training,
while momentary images of escape and John Wayne movies
are jarred by the eruption of airborne artillery.
Nowhere to hide but within this individual fortress
of sand and sticks and ammunition,
not knowing the cause, but the moment;
and the terror.
And the choices.
And the choices.
And the choices.
And the consequences ... and the unanswered questions.
Nothing to prepare you for the noise and repulsion.
Nothing to prepare you for the mental convulsion.
Nothing to prepare you for the sights and of death.
Nothing to prepare you for ... the choices.

Robert A. Toto, 10/31/1995

CHAPTER 18
GOING MY WAY

I'm sure this happens to most of us. When a mind seems devoid of current worries and stresses, it wanders back into the past, and suddenly there is an old memory as fresh and new as the day it occurred. In reliving this memory, you actually feel as if it is happening for the first time. In your mind, you know it's not a dream.

Such an occurrence recently happened to me about an event that happened almost forty years ago in South Vietnam. This following revisiting of my past is not fiction, and as I relive it and write it, I stand in awe of what transpired. My mother always said I had a good memory, and I can't disagree. I was born in 1947, and my earliest memories are from 1950. In the memory of what occurred in South Vietnam, I can isolate no specific date, but in looking at a calendar of 1971, the dates these events occurred are between 12/16/71 and 12/20/71. The following true story represents my transition from one who aspired to do, to a person who has accomplished a vital mission.

Heading South

By the second week of December 1971, my mission as a rather senior first lieutenant in Phu Bai had come to a successful conclusion. I was in my second full month in Vietnam, and my field duty in a combat zone was concluded. My mission had been to secure the eastern zone of an ASP (ammunition supply point) in Phu Bai to turn over to the South Vietnamese Army (ARVN) before the US Army departure from the area. At the time this mission was completed by my ragtag detachment of short-timers, I had no idea how important the accomplishment of this mission was. In the grand scheme of things, I later learned that it was a highly critical operation closely monitored by General Sweeney and his staff at his headquarters in Da Nang. Regardless, my job was done, and I received orders to report to the logistical support command in Da Nang. To me, this was the jackpot, for there were flush toilets and cold running water emanating from water coolers.

Yogi and Boo Boo

Sometime in the third week of December, I found myself in my company's orderly room, waiting the outgoing convoy making its daily run of Highway 1 through the Hai Van Pass. The first sergeant told me that the convoy wasn't leaving until around noon, which to me was an extraordinary waste of time. I needed to get to my next duty station at a much faster pace, and the sooner, the better. The fun began when two MACV (Military Assistance Command Vietnam) advisers walked into the orderly room. I have long since forgotten their names, so for this re-creation, let's call them Yogi and Boo Boo. Relatively senior captains in their late twenties, one was an African American and the other a Southern Caucasian with a deep Southern drawl. The way they talked to each other, with one trying to be funnier than the other, would have made a great stand-up comedy routine, hence my Yogi and Boo Boo moniker.

Follow the Yellow Brick Road!

Yogi and Boo Boo were taking their quarter ton to Da Nang by themselves, and as second-tour Vietnam vets of the infantry persuasion, they had no need for a secure convoy. In all my insecure impatience, I asked if I could come along, thus getting to Da Nang earlier. Little did I know that this scenic romp down the Hai Van Pass would certify Yogi and Boo Boo to be absolutely crazy, with different life goals and experiences than I possess.

These two characters would turn out to be the most memorable combat officers in my rather limited military career. I proceeded to get my duffel bag and put on my flak jacket. I grabbed my ancient snub-nosed M-1 rifle and was ready to go. I was in the back of the quarter ton, with Yogi driving and Boo Boo riding shotgun. I immediately knew I was in trouble when Yogi gunned the jeep and we proceeded down the winding and hilly Hai Van Pass as if we were racing in the Daytona 500. As we settled in for our scenic coastal trip, both Yogi and Boo Boo talked about their previous infantry assignments and how they compared to their current combat assignment as advisers to the ARVN. They questioned me on my field experience and stated unequivocally that I needed a field infantry tour to get the real taste of what Vietnam was all about. In essence, they were true military lifers who were not only schooled and experienced in combat but actually sought out more combat adventures.

These guys were little kids in a large playground created for their entertainment. They were living out their fantasies in central Vietnam as a walking recruitment poster, fighting communism and preventing the dreaded domino theory. On the other hand, in little over two years in the army, I can honestly say I had just completed my first honest-to-God true mission successfully, and I can say that it was the first time I felt I was a major contributor in a true military mission. Hence my sense of purpose and satisfaction were on the other end of the military spectrum of my two colleagues, who were going my way in a directional sense while I was going my own esoteric way.

A Sniper in the Hills

The weather seemed to improve as we moved south, and the sun was playing hide-and-seek as the mist from the South China Sea was starting to burn off the hills and valleys. Just as this was transpiring, the sound of popping noises started to emanate from the nearby passing hills. Yogi started laughing and accelerated the vehicle as it suddenly dawned on me that a VC sniper was taking aim at us. Boo

Boo laughed, saying this sniper couldn't hit the broad side of a barn. Obviously, this was not what I'd signed up for, and looking back at the mad set of moments, I can honestly say that it was surreal—something that did happen but which I refuse to believe occurred. Yogi and Boo Boo thought it hilarious; I, on the other hand, took these actions rather seriously. It was the first and only time that someone deliberately shot a weapon at me.

In the Oriental Mist

We descended from the pass, and the weather darkened. We entered a valley engulfed in an Oriental mist. In entering this low-lying stretch of land, I saw in the mist an incredible Buddha monument that had to be over three stories high, casting its shadow upon Highway 1. The mere sight of the magnificent structure made me aware that I was witnessing a way of life in a beautiful and ancient land where we were nothing but mere intruders as the ghosts of Oriental chronicles. That was when I took in the beauty of the land and realized that these people would continue life as they knew it after we occupying troops were long gone. Obviously, Yogi and Boo Boo's view of this country took on a different meaning to them.

Welcome to Rocket City

As we arrived at my next duty station compound in all its combat-like ugliness, as only the US Army can create, I thanked them and wished them good luck on their completion of their tours. As I walked to the orderly room for my next assignment, I took a deep breath and hoped that a stray bullet or rocket wouldn't prevent my return to "the world." However, the lesson I learned in following the "yellow brick road" of the Hai Van Pass with Yogi and Boo Boo is that we were temporary voyagers in a foreign land. I sensed the cultural beauty and sense of history while my traveling companions saw something entirely different in helping me in "going my way."

How strange this episode was, and I would love to take the trek again, without Yogi and Boo Boo, and see that beautiful section of the world along the winding road next to the South China Sea. Without

Yogi and Boo Boo, I would never have experienced this tour on the wild-side.

> *Father Fitzgibbons: "I'm sure the way to say what I'd like to say will occur to me after you've gone."*
> *(From the film Going My Way, circa 1944)*

CHAPTER 19
WAS THAT FORTY-ONE OR
FORTY-TWO ROCKETS?

My tour of Vietnam can be divided into two parts. I spent time in the field in Phu Bai and held down a staff job in the logistical command in Da Nang. My initial assignment in Vietnam was time in the primitive post of Phu Bai, where the battle cry rang "Phu Bai is all right," according to Hanoi Hannah. In this regard, I must admit that Phu Bai was a veritable haven in which American forces never faced the wrath of "Charlie." I remember the drabness of this military installation and that our compound was a semi-fortified slum location without hot water or flush toilets, and it reeked of a humid moldy smell that has never escaped my memory.

Also constant in this distant memory of forty years ago was the outgoing ordnance of harassing and interdiction firing of the 105 howitzer battery next to us. In fact, after a few nights of this steady cadence of outgoing shelling, the noise became a serenade that lulled me to sleep each night. It was rather remarkable that Phu Bai dished out pain to the VC, but the VC never attacked us. All my time in doing my highly prioritized mission in this remote hovel was accomplished in the miserable field conditions of the rainy monsoon season. In doing my mission, "Charlie" didn't bother me and Hanoi Hannah kept telling us "Phu Bai is all right." As far as I was concerned, these arrangements suited me well.

The Thrill of Having Flush Toilets!

After two months of life in the fields of Phu Bai, I was transferred to the logistical support command of Da Nang for staff duty. I soon found out the duties of my assignment, which was the charge of directing the equipment handed in by departing units standing down from Vietnam. Our office determined where all the assets would go—to such destinations as the South Vietnam Army (ARVN), Okinawa, or stateside. The job was mind-numbing and repetitive paperwork that I grinded out twelve hours a day, seven days a week, from late December of 1971 through March of 1972. The weather was changing from the rainy monsoon season to the warmer dry season. It was warm and humid but not quite the hot, sunny tropical climate that would follow late in the spring.

Our compound in Da Nang was all self-sustaining and included its own electric power, mess hall, medical facilities, and water purification facilities. I must also point out that these facilities had plumbing, hot water, flush toilets, and water coolers. After two months in Phu Bai, Da Nang seemed like a paradise in the middle of the desert.

The routine at the support base included having long workdays in sandbagged buildings without much ventilation. I woke up at 05:00 hours, had morning chow at 05:30, and reported for duty at 06:30. I usually worked without having lunch, due to the hot and humid climate conditions, and usually retired from my duties between 18:30 and 19:00 hours. By this time, dinner was usually taken at the officers' mess, and it was normal modus operandi that the bar was open and a movie was showing for the evening's entertainment. Most of us turned in at our hooches by 23:00 hours. By the next morning, the cycle would repeat itself ad nauseam and continue without end.

Mind-Numbing Routine

The staff work cycle continued all around us as we were reminded that the war was continuous all around us, as evidenced by the constant air chopper traffic in the skies and the constant incoming rockets each night. From sunup to sundown, the constant sound of *whop, whop,*

whop emanated as background noise for all to hear. Along with the acrid humid smells of Vietnam, the sound of close-range choppers and distant cobra gunships discharging ordnance made for an eclectic smorgasbord to all of our senses. With all this going on in the daily routine, the main concern for every command was basic security.

Local security to deter Charlie from infiltration and attack was of primary importance. Every day, all major roads were swept for mines and booby traps. All military vehicle gas caps were locked to prevent the VC from sabotaging a vehicle by taping a grenade closed and putting it in the gas tank. The tape would erode, and the grenade would explode, detonating the said vehicle. Life could be cut short if one wasn't vigilant. Even in supposed secure staff areas, the war was still in play and was not an area to let one's guard down.

Da Nang Equals Rockets!

In the first two weeks, we had sapper attacks and distant incoming rocket fire. When these occurrences happened, the siren would go off and we would scramble to the nearest sandbagged bunker. These were ugly dugouts in the earth, with no lights other than an occasional flashlight. Sitting in these rooms with our helmets and flak jackets was not my idea of a Southeast Asian vacation.

So you get the picture of our rather mundane yet somewhat disturbing routine. After a while, as one settles into this routine, it can affect one's nerves, and fatigue begins to set in. In early January of 1972, I was on that downward slope and wearing down. One night I turned in at around 23:00 hours, and as usual, I slept through the night and woke up at 05:00. I proceeded to the latrine to shower. I dressed and walked through the morning darkness and mist to the mess hall.

As I took my tray to my customary table, I was greeted by two of my officer peers, whom I'll call Jerry and Kramer. Jerry immediately questioned me rather abruptly. "Where the hell were you during the rocket attack?"

Kramer butted in and said, "Didn't you see the damage along the base perimeter?"

I looked at both of them as if they had three heads, saying rather sheepishly, "How many rockets?"

Kramer mumbled, "Forty-one or forty-two, I guess. I seemed to have lost count."

"Oh," I said, "I didn't hear anything."

Jerry screamed, "You didn't hear—seven or eight people were killed, and we have all that damage outside!"

At a loss for words, I merely said, "Well, Jerry, it's dark outside, and besides, I was dead tired. I didn't hear a thing!"

I missed all the excitement. All I can say about this remarkable incident is that it happened ... and I have no recollection of it. I'd slept through the attack. Some war, some excitement!

> *Oh, say can you see by the dawn's early light*
> *What so proudly we hailed at the twilight's last gleaming?*
> *Whose broad stripes and bright stars through the perilous fight,*
> *O'er the ramparts we watched were so gallantly streaming?*
> *And the rockets' red glare, the bombs bursting in air,*
> *Gave proof through the night that our flag was still there.*
>
> *I'll have to take their word for it!*

> *First Lieutenant Richard C. Geschke*

> *In Early January 1972 on that particular dawning morning I found myself humming The Star Spangled Banner.*

CHAPTER 20
INCOMING AT THE ROCKET CITY:
DA NANG IS ALL WRONG!

Wisdom from the Point
I met him in the zone;
There was a school in Vilseck
To learn the mysteries of CBR.
We were young and naive.
As a West Point graduate,
His ticket needed to be punched.
He roamed the hills of Da Nang,
Where he saw Charlie wreaking havoc.
Later, in an O-Club annex,
He said to me,
"Even though we were the grunts,
It was you who took the heat
For our lack of success!"
Related to me from a West Pointer

First Lieutenant Richard C. Geschke
Da Nang, circa March 1972

After sleeping through a major rocket attack, I took my own security and well-being very seriously. Living in Da Nang meant better facilities, with flush toilets and hot water. However, looking back on this period, this location was filled with hazards and potential life-ending traps in every phase of operations and daily routines. In assessing this time frame, I can relate to the mentality and culture of towns in the territories of the Wild West in North America during the late 1900s, where there was gambling, prostitution, and uncontrolled violence.

Another analogy would be to compare Da Nang to a Mexican border town. Da Nang and Juarez seemed to present similar vices to entice young men to risk everything for a good time. These vices included prostitution and drugs. The only thing the border town would lack would be the massive violence that was a daily staple when living in Da Nang during the war.

Da Nang is now and was then a large city located in the center of Vietnam. It served as both a major port city and harbored the busiest airport in the world during the height of the Vietnam hostilities. Of all the major target areas, including Saigon, Long Binh, and Cam Ranh, Da Nang had the most assets. Its air force base had the most aircraft anywhere in Southeast Asia. Consequently, this made Da Nang a major targeted area for the VC and the NVA (North Vietnamese Army), which presented a nightmare task to the armed forces as to how to secure the large area.

There was a multitude of army, navy, and air force compounds all over the Da Nang metropolitan area. The harbor, with its indigenous sampan traffic going in and around bridges and harbor facilities, provided a target-rich area for the VC to attack. The army had their corps headquarters in Da Nang, along with all the logistical and support commands that dictated the actions for all of I Corps. However, it was the air base that was the number one target for the VC. The air force had the most assets, which were located at Da Nang. A plethora of sorties flew out of Da Nang to attack North Vietnam and the Ho Chi Minh Trail, along with providing close air support to all US Army and ARVN military operations.

Richard C. Geschke and Robert A. Toto

Da Nang, February 1972
Bunker in foreground, Chinook chopper in background

The Night Belongs to Charlie

Once the sun set over the mountains of Vietnam, the saying was gospel to all GIs and ARVN troops: "The night belongs to Charlie. Late at night when you're sleeping, Charlie Cong comes a creepin' around!" As with all locations during the Vietnam War, it was at night that the enemy came out for the hunt. In Da Nang, Charlie's modus operandi was to infiltrate all the high points surrounding the city. One particularly popular area was located in the elevated hills of Monkey Mountain. It was from this location that the VC would fire off their rockets to their designated areas.

Truth be told, the VC had no FDC (fire direction center) to direct their fire. To the VC, it was a hit-or-miss proposition, so they would target certain areas and fire every night. The VC would never stay in one position too long for fear of being located and subjected to direct artillery fire from the Americans. Their tactics were hit-and-run all night long. Although the VC were eclectic in their target selection, their main target area each night was some part of the Da Nang Air Base.

American security was a basic and simple plan utilized throughout the metropolitan area of Da Nang. Infantry security companies were

192

assigned sectors throughout all perimeters and harbor and air base facilities. In the mountains surrounding Da Nang, infantry battalions constantly patrolled the hills around and adjacent to Monkey Mountain to intercept and destroy any VC operations. The streets of Da Nang were empty of all civilian and military activities except the MP (Military Police) patrols doing their security rounds. What the Americans were striving for in Da Nang was a quiet night. However, in reality, there were no quiet nights in Da Nang. Every night in Da Nang was like July 4th. Rockets reigned terror on some section of the city nightly after sundown.

To add to this rocket mentality, there were sappers trying to infiltrate secured compounds throughout the metropolitan area every night. The infantry security companies were constantly setting off flares in efforts to catch these infiltrators in the act. Sounds of small-arms fire, along with outgoing artillery fire and with incoming rockets searching for targets, were a nightly feature emanating from the auspices of "the rocket city." The night belonged to Charlie, and all the Americans were doing was safeguarding their assets, trying to prevent the VC from imposing their will on our operations.

The Life of a VC Ammo Bearer

There was a well-told story that circulated in Vietnam about the life of a VC ammo bearer who started his journey in North Vietnam, carrying two rockets to the Vietcong in South Vietnam. The dedicated soldier would pack only the bare necessities, including his ration of rice and his bowl. His main cargo was the two rockets carried on a sling around his shoulders as he advanced down the well-beaten Ho Chi Minh Trail, through the thick Laos jungles. On his trek, he encountered severe monsoon rains along with the trappings of malaria-bearing mosquitoes and deadly poisonous snakes. Intermittently, this soldier would see firsthand the B-52 bombings wreaking havoc up and down the trail. His adventures were terrorizing, but he was never deterred in accomplishing his mission: to deliver his two rockets to the VC located in South Vietnam. Much to his joy, he finally arrived at his destination and unpacked his much-needed cargo.

> *The local VC rocket launcher receives the rounds and immediately fires off the two rounds bound for US installation targets. The local VC rocket launcher turns to the dedicated ammo bearer and says, "Well, what are you waiting for? Go back and get me two more rockets!"*

The story was told as a joke, but that was the type of enemy we were facing. They were determined to maintain their way of life. No amount of our forced will was ever going to change the minds, attitudes, or the culture of these people. This was their country. Come hell or high water, no matter how long we stayed there or tried to change their way of life or their attitudes, the more determined and hostile they became. We couldn't stay there forever, and they knew it!

Tempting Fate

Most personnel in Da Nang lived in Class 3 facilities. The living arrangements were not homelike; however, they presented no real hardship. The staff routines for most officers and men consisted of working twelve to fourteen hour a day, seven days a week.

It was amazing to me that many of the staff officers felt that they had to partake in the nightlife of Da Nang. This meant their actions were in direct disobedience of the nightly curfew. No American soldier was to be outside any military base in Da Nang after sundown.

It seemed to me that the majority of the curfew offenders were married men. Almost every night, these men would leave the compound before sundown, and the next time you would see them was either at the latrine showers the next morning or at the mess hall eating breakfast. Where did they go, you ask? Most of them went to the local brothels to drink and whore the entire night long. Others would go to local betting establishments for card and crap games. One thing was immensely clear: they were all in danger.

From my personal experiences, I knew of five men who were killed while frequenting a whorehouse. The VC booby-trapped the facility, and it killed all the Americans, along with the prostitutes. The facility was located half of a kilometer from the base, and it was completely destroyed. This wasn't an isolated occurrence. While I was stationed in Da Nang, this happened multiple times. In fact, it got me thinking of just how the army handled informing the next of kin of the death of these troopers. Were they given Purple Hearts for suffering "wounds from hostile enemy action?" I'm sure they didn't hear the truth. It probably was a touching boilerplate condolence letter. If the truth were told, this is how the letter should be written:

Dear Mr. and Mrs. X:
> *We regret to inform you of your son's death in Madam X's Whorehouse, where he was killed by a local VC detachment. Please be informed that he felt no pain and was rather enjoying his last activities on Earth.*

Respectfully,
Captain X

Many soldiers in Da Nang insisted on pushing the envelope and tempting fate. Even without tempting fate, Da Nang was nothing but a gigantic crapshoot. If you were careless, the penalty was death. You didn't have to partake in the dangerous nightlife of Da Nang to be killed; all you had to do was drive a vehicle. These dangers were all too real when negotiating the streets of Da Nang. One never knew in the daylight hours who were the friendlies and who were the foes.

Taking a Stroll in a Da Nang Compound

It was mid-February, and I was in my second full month of performing the duties of my staff job in Da Nang. Rarely did I leave my assigned staff building, but on this particular day, the weather began to change. It was becoming much more humid, and the sun was beating down on all the heavily sandbagged buildings. It was approximately 14:00 hours and I was in search of something cold to drink with ice. The only place I knew to get it was at the officers' mess hall just down the road. It was only about a half mile, and I decided to walk since the jeep was being utilized by Captain P, my boss. As I started down the compound road, which was asphalt, there was the usual high volume of trucks traveling with their assigned cargos. I must have walked about four hundred meters, when all of a sudden, about seventy-five meters in front of me, a deuce and a half truck exploded. All I can remember doing was hitting the pavement as I watched in horror the burning truck in front of me.

I looked around to see if there was any enemy activity, such as the shooting of weapons. No weapons had been fired. What the hell happened? The vehicle hadn't taken a rocket hit, and in my immediate terror, it did not occur to me that the truck was the victim of the taped hand grenade booby-trap device. All I ever heard were the stories and the warnings; never did I realize that I would see such happenings firsthand in combat. My heart was beating fast as all of us rushed to the burning vehicle. What amazed me was that the two personnel in the truck actually survived. They were blown out of the vehicle, through the front window and onto the pavement in front of them. Both of them had severely lacerated head injuries, but they did survive. The vehicle immediately stopped upon explosion and did not move forward to run over the troopers. Even in broad daylight, Charlie was omnipresent. Life in Da Nang was hazardous to one's health, and one never knew how the enemy would strike. I just realized that I never got that cold drink; instead, I returned rather shaken to my assigned staff building.

Just What the Hell Are We Doing Here?

I spent three months doing staff work in Da Nang. What the heck is staff work, and just what did we do for twelve to fourteen hours a day in a sandbagged non-air-conditioned building? My answer to this question is the term you have heard before: Vietnamization. Nixon's program was going forth with gusto, and units were being disbanded with the colors (unit insignias) being returned to active stateside duty or being deactivated (put in mothballs). My mission at Phu Bai was the cause of many units to DEROS (date eligible for return from overseas). By accomplishing my Phu Bai mission, units were standing down as excess in the Vietnamization process. Many units were going home, and the units quite literally were disbanded. In the orderly withdrawal of units of the US Army, it was the responsibility of the property book officers to make a complete inventory of all the physical assets of each and every unit.

Once that inventory was completed, the assets were divided into two major categories. The categories were labeled pima (primary assets) and secondary (secondary assets). Our job at the staff level was to assess each unit's property book and to break down the assets accordingly to the major categories of pima and secondary. Once this was accomplished, we were given a set priority of which assets needed to be filled in Southeast Asia and in the Pacific theater. It became immediately apparent that the Vietnamese Army was to be given the highest priority for the newest and best assets. I actually started to curse my own actions in Phu Bai. I discovered that a plethora of units were in DEROS mode from Phu Bai due to the accomplishment of my mission.

The floodgates of Vietnamization were open, and my meager staff of eight enlisted men along with another officer was responsible for earmarking millions of dollars of assets to be destined to Okinawa, the continental United States, and to the ARVN. It soon became apparent that the majority of pima equipment that was in excellent to good condition was sent directly to the ARVN. If I had to guess as to the percentage of high-market items that ended up with the ARVN, it would be at 95 percent. It got to be downright embarrassing when the ARVN became so demanding that they would not take a jeep with a slight crack in the windshield. It became the modus operandi that the ARVN were to be treated on a higher plain. That's when I knew that our so-called allies were nothing but spoiled brats. They had no concept of their mission or how they were to accomplish it! In the grand scheme of things, we could have given the ARVN the world, but never in one hundred years would they be able to rid themselves of the hostile actions of the North Vietnamese and the VC—no way!

Going Back to Phu Bai

With so many units standing down, our tiny office was severely swamped with demands from outgoing units to make the final disposition on assets. Captain P was desperate to stand down the majority of the units in Phu Bai and not to wait for the normal flow of paperwork to make its way slowly to our shop. His orders were direct and simple. He gave me a list of pima equipment and destinations, along with the order to make on-the-spot decisions directing where the secondary assets would go. I was to head out by chopper the next morning at 06:30 hours and spend the whole day in Phu Bai, making sure that the ten units on stand-down orders were completely dealt with.

That morning, as we headed north to Phu Bai, I saw the most beautiful sunrise of my life. Heading north and looking east to the South China Sea and west onto the lush green jungles and winding rivers and rice paddies, I realized that when it was not enduring the monsoons, this area was truly a magnificent sight. Another thing I noticed was that the route of the chopper was a true zigzag route with constant elevation changes to avoid any leading fire from the enemy. By the end of the flight, my stomach was queasy, and I had a touch of vertigo. As we arrived at the helipad, I got off the chopper and looked around. My God, it wasn't raining.

I quickly got to work and made my on-the-spot decisions. I was able to clear all ten of the stand-down units' property books. My chopper was leaving at 18:30 hours, and I wasn't going to miss it. I knew that Hanoi Hannah was zeroing in the rockets on Da Nang, and that in the same breath she would say, "Phu Bai is all right!" I boarded the chopper just as the sun was beginning to nosedive by the Ashau Valley. That's the last time I saw Phu Bai.

As Dusk Settles in Da Nang

Have you ever been in the position of being where you weren't supposed to be? Well, I'm sure that most of us would answer in the affirmative. In Da Nang, such an answer would not bode well for the well-being of any trooper. Unfortunately, I am the culprit of the foregoing tale of woe, which only shows my propensity to push the envelope beyond the reasons of good sensibilities. My good boss Captain P gave me a window of opportunity, from 15:00 hours to 17:00 hours, to visit the local PPX (Pacific post exchange) to procure a stereo system for my brother. In all generosity, I was given a jeep, and I went my merry way along the major avenues of Da Nang, armed only with my .45-caliber sidearm.

It took me a good hour to select the components for my brother, and I paid the invoice with MPC and headed out to my jeep. As I traveled along the main highway among the local mopeds and lambrettas, I noticed that my jeep was listing to the front right, and that I had incurred a flat tire. It was nearing 18:30 hours, and it would be dark when I finished the task of fixing the flat. Remember, the night belonged to Charlie, and I only had a handful of rounds in the magazine of my .45-caliber weapon. I was approximately one mile from my destination, and I made the conscience decision to ride on that flat tire and hub to prevent my stopping and exposing myself to any VC actions. I ruined the wheel of the jeep, but I saved myself. The maintenance NCO was initially pissed, but when I explained the circumstances, he understood.

These Guys Are Drug Heads!

When I first arrived on my job in Da Nang, I became rather amused at the talk and griping of the enlisted men in my shop. The constant complaining was mostly about army chow, and the main lament was that once work was done, what do you do? Of the eight enlisted men, I quickly realized that I had four men who were definite "juicers" (drinkers of alcoholic beverages), and the other four were using drugs. At first, my suspicions of the drug users were only hunches. At times, a druggie's speech would be slow and introspective, almost to the point of sometimes being slurred. Whether they were juicers or suspected druggies, they did their jobs in general, and I had no problems other than hearing their constant griping about how tough they had it.

I came close several times to giving the old "just-be-lucky-you're-not-out-in-the-elements-of-the-field" speech. I held my tongue at these staffers' gripes and only insisted that my men accurately get their work done as quickly as possible. Sometimes, upon inspection of their reports, I would find inaccuracies, and I would have them redo it all, sometimes at the expense of their own time (and my time as well). Many nights I would have them correcting mistakes until 21:00 hours.

We closed shop every night and headed for our respective mess halls for evening chow. Most of the time in Da Nang, I would have breakfast and work through the noon hour with periodic breaks for water or coffee—such was the daily routine. I didn't eat lunch as the weather became warmer, for I had no appetite in the South Asian humidity. In the evening, I ate dinner at the officers' mess and met my staff officer peers for drinks and an open-air movie. Three nights out of seven, we never saw the end of the movie, as Charlie would be firing his rockets from Monkey Mountain as we scrambled to the bunkers. God how I hated the musty smell of the bunker as we sat and counted the number of projectiles that landed in the general area of Da Nang. This became a "Rocket City ritual" in which the VC orchestrated the night's activities and as sheep being led by the herder, we followed suit.

This routine continued through February and into March. Several of the enlisted men were getting "short" (less than thirty days left in Vietnam), with two in particular beginning to act abnormally. As I related, I suspected at least four of my enlisted men to be indulging in the use of drugs. During the middle of March, I detected two of my men acting strangely; they were unable to focus on their duties and were sweating profusely. After one such day of observation, I stayed behind when the staff left for the day. I confess that I searched the desks of the two troopers who were acting in an odd way. I found letters from both of these soldiers, explaining to their closest confidants that they were indeed trying to detox themselves in order to pass the urine test at the Da Nang replacement depot (repo depot). Both guys were junkies!

As their immediate superior, I was responsible for making sure that my superiors also knew of the activities of these enlisted men. When I told Captain P that these two troopers were indeed addicted to heroin, he refused to believe me. I told him that I understood his denial but to do me a favor and truly observe their actions over the next several days. Within forty-eight hours, Captain P confronted me and stated that the soldiers were officially ordered to a thirty-day detox program in Da Nang. Both troopers would have to wait before going back to "the world." It was a hard and fast rule at the time that no soldier was to return to the United States while addicted to drugs. The same was also true for venereal disease. It was well known that in Southeast Asia, there were several strains of VD that were very difficult to eradicate. Many a soldier had to extend his time in country while being treated for VD with powerful antibiotics.

With a Little Help from My Friends

At the end of January, I got a surprising in-country telephone call from Bob, who was at the Cam Ranh Bay Air Base. I asked him jokingly if he had transferred to the air force. Much to my surprise, Bob's voice was cracking as he told me he was headed home under the new policy of early "drops" (time in country being waived) for qualified personnel attending graduate school. Well, lucky me. Bob was going home, Couch was still in Germany, and I was dodging rockets and booby traps in Vietnam.

From late January until I left for home in April, I felt like the Lone Ranger. Since Stickney was still in Phu Bai, I didn't even have Tonto as a sidekick. Going on with my mind-numbing routine each day and night in "Rocket City," I became so brazen as to not always evacuate when the rockets were incoming. Why didn't I go to the safety of the bunker? My reasons were simple: first, I didn't like the sight or smell of a sandbagged bunker; second, I became an expert at knowing if the rockets were anywhere close to hitting us. If they started to zero in on our compound, I would hightail it to the bunker; otherwise, pour another drink, please! And so the beat goes on!

By the first week of March of 1972, the rumors were flying all about the base as units were standing down, and there seemed to be an excess of soldiers. The army was in the full swing of the Vietnamization program. Soldiers started to get early drops to return home and to be reassigned or separated from service. While everyone was going home, there I was, still in the Republic of Vietnam. One night in the middle of March, I was smoking my favorite cigar, the wood-tipped Hav-A-Tampa Jewel, talking with a fellow staff officer and my CO, Captain P. We were discussing the value of medals awarded in the combat zone of Vietnam, and out of nowhere, Captain P asked me if I had been put in for a Bronze Star Medal for meritorious service for my leadership in the preparations of the fortifications around the Phu Bai ASP. I said, "Sir, the thought never occurred to me."

The good captain was rather blunt and stated, "Lieutenant Geschke, you deserve a Bronze Star for your actions. The whole support command was following your every move in completing your task. Every weekly staff meeting conducted by General Sweeney included progress reports of the fortifications at Phu Bai. It was the top priority of command."

Within the week, Captain P and I attended a rather informal open officers' mess, where I met a West Point captain whom I knew from Vilseck, Germany. As was standard protocol, I introduced myself and got ready to see General Sweeney. The good captain said to me, "How are you doing, Geschke? The general is deeply indebted to you for your leadership in Phu Bai. He's putting you in for the Bronze Star. Don't fuck it up!" Really, I had no idea.

The Letter Home

7 March 72
Dear family,
I've made my decision to come home at the end of the month. I've got twenty-one days to go in Vietnam. It'll take me a couple of days to process out of Ft. Lewis, Washington. I'll fly out of Seattle to Cleveland.

It's weird to be getting out of the army. This has been my life for the last two and a half years! Right now, I'm just as uncertain and scared of getting out of the army as I was getting into the army. It's the fear of the unknown and one's future that makes one dubious.

It's going to be a strange feeling to finally come home after thirty months of traveling halfway around the world!! I'm definitely a changed person. I've seen the world and many of the people who comprise it. I wouldn't trade that for a million dollars! Many people my age have no idea of what I've seen and experienced, either good or bad. I guess many people back in the States don't know what it is to go on an alert in the freezing cold of Germany or the heat of Vietnam. They don't know what it's like to eat c-rations, which were cold, and be grateful for it. I guess they don't know what it is to wait for mail from home, which is your only communication with the outside world!! I guess a civilian wouldn't understand what it's like to live in the jungle like I did in Panama, when you found yourself chest high in a swamp, cussing. I just guess they won't understand what I saw in Vietnam—the people—the places and the war.

It's hard to explain things like I've mentioned without experiencing it yourself. I know a lot of my friends who are in the army now or who were in the army know what it's all about. However, there are a lot of people who just don't know!! All they know is their dull nine-to-five routine, their TV shows, their material well-being, which is to keep up with the Joneses. For some people, this is all they have done all of their lives. They are in their little world, and they have no real concept of what the rest of the world is doing. Many of these people will be the people I'll be associated with when I get back—some of them are my own friends.

So you see, I'll never regret being in the army. It was an experience I'll never forget. I've met people who have become some of my best friends, and I've met people I wouldn't give the time of day. But all in all, this is something I've experienced, and it will never be taken away from me. God bless.

Love,
Dick

Within the week, I also received my drop orders. The orders read that I was to DEROS on April 1, 1972. Hell, that was April Fools' Day. How could I trust the US government? On March 28, I headed in a jeep toward Da Nang Air Force Base. I checked into the repo depot and experienced the joys of processing out, which included the urinalysis check for drug use. As it happened, many of the enlisted men flunked their urinalysis tests and were sent directly from the repo depot to the rehab center in Da Nang. All juicers of the infantry ilk passed; however, they were very drunk in the interim. The drug users stayed for rehab; the juicers boarded and traveled the distance home. The next day, we were given our flight assignment and time of boarding. As a final test, they did a second urinalysis check to catch anyone at the repo depot. It was a known fact that the local mama-sans were selling pure heroin on the base. Damned if they didn't catch nine enlisted men using. Nine more soldiers making the ride to the rehab center. Then and there, I knew that there was a major drug problem in Vietnam.

This Bird's Headed Home!

By 15:00 on March 29, I was given my boarding pass, which I put in my duffel bag. We were told to change into Class A TWs, which were lightweight dress khaki uniforms. That afternoon, all our duffel bags were inspected for contraband, such as weapons or any other army-related equipment. German shepherds also sniffed all the outgoing baggage for drugs. Before embarking on the bus that would take us to the plane, we exchanged our MPC (military payment certificates) for US greenbacks. That's when it finally dawned on me that I was going home!

As the bus headed out of the repo depot, I was looking at the setting sun as it descended on Monkey Mountain in a reddish light purple haze. Night was beginning to fall on the Rocket City, and all I could think was, *get me to that damned plane*. Stories of planes being rocketed when trying to take off were common stories of lore in Vietnam. I didn't need any last-minute adventures. As luck would have it, no such thing occurred, and at approximately 19:30 hours, the plane took off, headed due east. Not until we leveled off at our flight elevation was a word said or spoken. It was eerily quiet. Once we leveled off, a loud cheer emanated from all concerned. This bird's headed home!

First Lieutenant Geschke
Da Nang, December 31, 1971

First Lieutenant Geschke, February 1972

CHAPTER 21
POST US ARMY: SOME WELCOME HOME

═══════════════════════════════════

A Toto Chapter

─────────────────────────────────

I was at Ft. Lewis and headed back to Massachusetts. When I'd left Cam Ranh, it was over ninety degrees, and I was wearing my TWs. It was the end of January, and it had snowed eighteen inches two days before I landed at Logan Airport. My mother and father greeted me in Boston, and we headed north toward our home on the New Hampshire border. I was damn tired.

I slept on real sheets that night, and I don't remember sleeping that well since I'd left Germany. There was snow everywhere, and I spent the next few days getting used to the weather and being a civilian again. My family threw me a welcome-home party, during which I preceded to get drunk. My mother forgave me that time.

Good thing my family and close friends were there to welcome me home. I can't say that of most of the other acquaintances and most civilians I encountered. I didn't have much downtime, which was the fault of paperwork arriving late. In just three days, I had to report to the campus of the University of Massachusetts Graduate School.

First things first. I made a call to Mr. and Mrs. Carl Geschke in Cleveland. I told them that I had talked to Dick three days before, and that he was well. I don't remember if my voice cracked, but as I spoke to the tough-minded steel worker from Republic Steel, he thanked me for the phone call and welcomed me home. I promised him I would write Dick often, and that I would pray for his safe return. Mrs. Geschke was a religious woman and said that Richard needed all the help that he could get. I agreed with that.

George Carlin said in his autobiography: "Weird how the military touches so many aspects of your life … You hate it but it forms you …" In his own biting way, Carlin was right. I don't know if it's the young age of the typical serviceman, or being away from all the "familiar" elements of home, but it does have a pronounced effect on your being. Besides the obvious regimen of doing things the "military way," it molds you in a manner that you don't expect. Perhaps it's the need to attach to something, perhaps it's the bond of friendship, perhaps it's the will to survive, but it is very powerful.

Being away from that environment, I was thrust into the realm of civilian-ship. In the military, you shared everything—thoughts, fears, cigarettes, food … everything. Now I was on my own. I could eat when I wanted, sleep when I wanted, and do nothing if I wanted. I had freedom of choice, but I secretly missed my comrades and feared for their safety.

Adjusting to Civilian Life

As I started graduate school, I felt out of place. I was surrounded by students who were just starting to emerge from their cocoons of adolescence. Almost none of my fellow graduate students had had the experiences of the military or going to war. But there I was, and I tried to adapt to the rigors of university life.

I thought about Dick all the time and wondered how he was doing. A piece of me wanted to be with him, but that was not possible. I became somewhat aloof with my classmates. My roommate was a decent guy, a history major, who had a great quality of listening to my many stories. He also introduced me into the writings of Saul Alinski. He was a savior of sorts. I had made one or two good male friends, and I proceeded to find my way through the labyrinth of university life.

Misconceptions of Who We Are

I had decided to return to my parents' home every weekend because something inside me wouldn't let go of the past. After about one month, one of my newly acquired friends talked me into staying the weekend to attend a party at a local girls' college—the names are excluded to protect the guilty.

At this time, I was approaching twenty-seven years of age. I attended this party of eighteen- to twenty-two-year-olds. The party was at its apex when I arrived. I grabbed a beer and leaned against a wall as these students did their *Animal House* routines. Almost on cue, a cute female from the college started to have a conversation with me. She asked all the usual questions and then asked me what I had been doing lately (as she knew I was a graduate student).

I told her that I had just returned from Vietnam and was pursuing an MBA degree at UMass. Suddenly, the atmosphere changed. She asked me, "How did it feel to kill women and children?" Well, let me tell you that I did everything in my power to refrain from smacking the bitch. What right did she even have to bring up the subject? She had no clue about the environment that we were subjected to, and she had chosen to ask a question about which she knew nothing.

I gritted my teeth and walked away from the woman. I sought out my friend who had acquired the invitation and told him I was leaving. He tried to convince me to stay, but my mind had made an irreversible decision, and I left without knowing how I was to get back to my room because my friend had the car. My friend came to the rescue, and I left the party.

In Germany, I had met many women. The vast majority were casual acquaintances, but some were not casual. (Pardon me as I pause to exhale.) While studying for finals in one of my courses, I received a letter from a special lover from my past. I had not heard from her in a while. She was returning to the States and wanted to meet me in New York. I was shell-shocked. After several agonizing hours, I wrote to her and told her no. She had already pierced my heart, and I was not prepared for her to do it again. I remembered the Dear John letter that Dick had received at Fort Benning. It was déjà vu, but not all over again, as Yogi Berra would say. We were hardened but not without emotion. I was pretty vulnerable at that time.

It Wasn't Easy!

I prepared to move on. At graduate school, there were some decent people. I encountered an interesting woman who was a fellow classmate. I tried to connect with her, but my attitude wasn't good; I clearly wasn't ready for a relationship. I sincerely hope that she found her "Lancelot."

I concentrated on my subjects and dove into academia. We had some terrific teachers and some losers, which in reality reflected what life was in general, that is taking the good with the bad. I thought about leaving graduate school, but the employment situation did not allow for that kind of flexibility. Unemployment was at a high level, and I did not need that kind of pressure.

Then there was the stigma of being a Vietnam veteran. Not only did we not have a welcome home, but we were also treated as a disease—a boil upon the populace. A contagious disease that had to be eradicated. A cancerous spot on the mind that must be eradicated to destroy the roots. What had we done to deserve this treatment? I thought that we had been serving our country. The country was trying to forget our participation, and we were testimony to the fact that people were still dying in an undeclared war. I remember Lyndon Johnson saying, "It gives me no pleasure to send the flower of our youth into harm's way …" Maybe he understood that the "buds" of the flowers were real people dying to maintain our passion for freedom.

After I finished one term of graduate school, I was ready to find myself in the glory of the employed. After several months of unsuccessful searching, I finally landed a job with a local company as an assistant office manager. It was as if all that I had been through was a mirage. People went to work with the blasé attitude of an uninterested observer. Vietnam was an inconvenient blip in history. Tell that to the over fifty thousand people who gave their lives.

Richard C. Geschke and Robert A. Toto

As True Veterans, We Learned to Adjust

Soon afterward, I met my wife on a blind date. She said that I sounded taller on the phone, and she wore high heels on our first date. She had been told that I had recently returned from Vietnam. While not a warmonger, I think that she had a better grasp of the situation than most people did. She had volunteered to attend dances at the local USO in California, where she met several returning Vietnam veterans. She has a gift for listening and patience that I can only dream about. She turned out to be a lifelong partner and friend. Dick and Ann Geschke are still part of our civilian life. Attendance at weddings and get-togethers was part of the bonding that Dick and I went through, and their friendship is embodied in our spirit.

I hope that the reader will not attack us for our candor or our zeal for relating our memories. I know that we have tried to be accurate in our facts, but emotion sometimes gets in the way. Former President Lyndon Johnson wrote a book called *Vantage Point*, in which he tried to explain events as seen through his vantage point. I have read the book from cover to cover, and I saw the no-win situation that he tragically felt. It obviously led to his decision not to run for another term, which I think was the first time in history that a sitting president did not run for office during a wartime situation. *Note from Geschke: Due to the actions of General MacArthur, Truman did not run for president again either.*

Dick and I have been through some mind-numbing events over the last forty years. Unemployment, parents dying, relocation of our families, the birth of our children and now this treatise, which I hope the reader will find entertaining. Some parts were perfect, some were gut wrenching, some were painful, and some were fulfilling.

We are the baby boomers of the men who went to war and the women who held it together until the men returned. Every marketing manager has tried to exploit this wave of boomers and find the right solution of just what this generation wants to do to satisfy their needs.

The solution is ever so simple. It is the human spirit and the force to overcome all obstacles. George Carlin was right—the military did change us. We were young, sometimes brave, and sometimes stupid.

210

But we felt for our common man at a time when our common people punished the bad along with the good.

God bless our military. God bless America.

Robert Toto in civilian attire Amsterdam 1970

CHAPTER 22
RETURN TO THE WORLD!

I had a window seat, and as I looked out on the horizon, the sun was setting in the west. Soon it would be dark. Our first destination was Okinawa. When we landed, we changed crews for the first time. Onward east we went, and the sun rose again as we circled above Pearl Harbor to land in Hawaii. Another crew change and off we went to our final destination of McCord Air Force Base in Seattle, Washington. With this leg, the sun set again. We had been in the air for a total of eighteen hours. As we touched down at McCord, it was about 02:30 Pacific time on the morning of March 30, 1972.

I was dog-tired as we disembarked from the plane. Some of the troopers knelt down and kissed the tarmac. I remember the chill of the spring Washington morning, and I had no inclination to bend down and kiss the earth of "Uncle Sam." Get me to a bed! At about 04:00 hours, I was zonked out and, rather "army-like," was rudely awakened at 06:00 hours to get my "sorry ass out of bed" and proceed to morning chow! Yes, I still was in the army. We shaved, showered, and went to eat.

Preparing to go Home

At 08:00 hours, we were processing out of the army. Paperwork was prepared first, and this took three hours. Waiting in line and proceeding forward, we had to have physical exams. Once the administrative paperwork and examination were complete, it was time for afternoon chow. I was seated in the waiting room, and an E-4 was moving around the room, giving tickets for the steak dinner to all returning personnel from Vietnam. As the specialist continued around the room, he gave the tickets for the dinner to Vietnam returnees only. A lieutenant who served in Alaska did not receive a dinner ticket. This lieutenant from Alaska objected about not being included as a dinner guest. The E-4 dutifully explained that only returning veterans from a combat zone were given the steak dinner. He began to complain that it was unfair. I looked at him and said, "Where the fuck were you when I took the trip to Nam and had to deal with Charlie? Just be grateful that you're going home!" It's funny—he didn't say one word!

Once I had my steak dinner, I headed out to the admin area to receive my DD-214. These were my discharge papers, which I have to this very day. They are records of all the time I spent on active duty, including all my duty stations, medals, and citations earned. At that particular time, I had no idea that I would receive the Bronze Star. My Bronze Star was in process, so it was not included in my DD-214. It was March 31, 1972, and my Bronze Star was signed and sealed in Vietnam on April 1, 1972. In retrospect, I should have my DD-214 amended to include the Bronze Star. My DD-214 can be amended and I shall do so. Bronze star or not, all I wanted to do at that moment was get my butt on a plane and head home to Cleveland.

My plans were to take residence in a local hotel and get some much-needed rest. I was exhausted. I headed to the nearest phone booth to call home and tell my parents that I was at Fort Lewis and was traveling home the next day. My father answered the phone and immediately asked where I was. I told him I was in Fort Lewis, and that I was headed to a hotel to get some sleep. I said I would be getting a flight the next morning for Cleveland. General Geschke immediately canceled all such plans and said, "You get your ass on a plane today and get home as fast as possible, even if you have to travel all night!" There was no arguing with my father, and I told him I would get the next available flight home. I was to call him later to give him the estimated time of arrival in Cleveland. I took a taxi to the Seattle airport and got military standby tickets for a red-eye flight headed to Chicago at 23:30 hours. I had eight hours to kill at the airport after I called my father with the arrival details.

Where's My Ticket?

The USO had a lounge rest area where I could get snacks and beverages and also a bed to catch some much-needed sleep. I immediately fell asleep and had been out for six hours when one of the USO girls shook me awake. She said that they were beginning to board the plane for my flight. I thanked her and immediately rummaged through my duffel bag for my airplane ticket. I couldn't find it anywhere. My heart sank as I searched everywhere. As the final calls for boarding were announced, I struggled to the ticket counter with my pitiful story of woe. I guess they'd seen exhausted GIs lose their tickets, because they let me board the plane. Two and a half years of challenges and tests, and within only half a day, I could have blown my triumphant return home because I lost a plane ticket! Go figure!

I boarded a brand new DC-10, which was quite a large plane, second only to the 747s, which were the largest of the commercial jets at that time. Regardless of what type of plane it was, I flopped into my assigned seat and promptly fell asleep. As I arrived at Chicago's O'Hare airport for the second time in my life, I found myself rushing through the terminal as I had five months prior, looking for my connecting flight to Cleveland. Alas, another DC-10 and I was going home. To tell you the truth, I couldn't fall asleep. It was about 09:00 hours when we took off, headed toward Hopkins International Airport. I landed on a gray, overcast day in the lands of the Western Reserve of Connecticut on April 1, 1972. Goddamn, I was home!

I struggled with my duffel bag as I headed to the outgoing passenger area, where my father was waiting for me in his car. My father was known to be a tough steelworker who spent thirty years of his life in the flats of the industrial hub of Cleveland. He was the smartest of any man I had ever met. His education was formed on the streets of Cleveland; he was well read and possessed a PhD in "life." In other words, he had street smarts. The old man drove a Volkswagen, and he immediately opened the front trunk so I could stuff my duffel bag in it. He told me that I looked like shit, but regardless, he was driving to the Marriot Hotel where my mother worked. Needless to say, mom cried! Dad was protective of Mom, and come hell or high water, because I was the firstborn, this reuniting was an important ritual. I'll never forget it. It was like the prodigal son returning home!

Home in Cleveland

I served my country for almost thirty months. During that time span, I never had a PCS (permanent change of station) in the continental United States. I've trained in the States, but all my real-time assignments were overseas. Having spent all my military acumen overseas, I was indeed a veteran trooper. I was a crusty "old salt." Believe me, as I entered the grounds of the West Park section of my parents' home in Cleveland, I was one tired dude!

To my surprise, Carl F. Geschke treated me as a true veteran. After coming home, my nights in Cleveland were days and my days were nights. During this period, my body was trying to recover from all the stress and strain of the last two and a half years. To be honest, I never slept so much in all my life. My time clock took some time to adjust. Within two months, my rhythms did change. I did gain some weight, but my social skills, especially with the females, were in a sorry state. During this period of American history, if you were a Vietnam veteran, the first and foremost rule of engagement with the female sex was never to tell her that you served in Vietnam. Most women of this generation shunned such a man back then. In looking back at this, I find this behavior revolting.

For the next ten years of my life, we as Vietnam veterans were shown the raw end of the deal. We as soldiers were not advocates of the conflict; we were only the players who were doing their civic duties. In time, this would go away, but I never truly forgot the utter sense of abandonment that I realized during this period. It wasn't until many years later that the Vietnam vet was regarded in the positive vein that should have occurred immediately.

Within the first week of my arrival in Cleveland, there was a packet sent from Da Nang, Vietnam. I opened it at the kitchen table of my parents' home. Inside was my citation from General Arthur

H. Sweeney, Jr., Major General, USA Commanding The Bronze
Star Medal To First Lieutenant Richard C Geschke ——— Infantry
United States Army.

Citation
By Direction Of The President
The Bronze Star Medal
Is Presented To
First Lieutenant Richard C. Geschke ——— Infantry
United States Army

*Who distinguished himself by outstandingly meritorious
service in connection with military operations against a hostile
force in the Republic of Vietnam. During the period*

November 1971 To March 1972
*He consistently manifested exemplary professionalism and
initiative in obtaining outstanding results. His rapid assessment
and solution of numerous problems inherent in a combat
environment greatly enhanced the allied effectiveness against
a determined and aggressive enemy. Despite many adversities,
he invariably performed his duties in a resolute and efficient
manner. Energetically applying his sound judgment and extensive
knowledge, he has contributed materially to the successful
accomplishment of the United States mission in the Republic
of Vietnam. His loyalty, diligence and devotion to duty were in
keeping with the highest traditions of the military service and
reflect great credit upon himself and the United States Army.*

I'd handed the citation to my father. He read it and said nothing at
all. All I remember was a shake of the head and his handing it over to
my mother. Mom was not so subtle when she said, "Richard, I think
your letters to us didn't tell the whole story!"

I started to job hunt, and by May of 1972, I secured a teaching
position at a Catholic school, where I taught seventh- and eighth-grade
social studies. I was hired for the 1972–73 school year, beginning in
September. In essence, I had the whole summer to do as I wished. In
looking back now, I realize that it was the only true vacation I ever
had.

Over the next thirty-eight years, I would never take more than one week at a time off. I traveled to Massachusetts to see Bob in the summer of 1972, and we headed out to the local haunts and even took in a baseball game at Fenway Park. I returned home, and before I knew it, I was teaching history and geography to seventh and eighth graders. It was at this time that I met my future wife. We dated for more than a year and got married in December of 1973. Toto was the best man at my wedding. The next year was his turn, and he married Paulette. As luck would have it, we're still married all these years later.

Since I was a teacher in a parochial school with hardly any benefits and with a low salary structure, I taught for only one year. By the summer of 1973, I gave my notice to the school that I would not renew my contract. Since most of the best school systems were not hiring and only offered substitute teaching positions, I had to look elsewhere to make a living. I was now engaged to my future wife, Ann, and I had to be gainfully employed.

By September of 1973, I was working as a senior accountant at a Mack Trucks, Inc. factory branch. To this day, I work as a controller in the automotive industry. As we shifted into civilian life, Bob and I had to deal with a tight economy and a new corporate attitude that had taken hold. Large companies were no longer benevolent benefactors of the good life. Throughout the seventies and into the eighties, the workplace culture changed. It became dog-eat-dog. That fact hit home to me when the industrial base that was prevalent in Cleveland dried up along with all the good-paying jobs.

It forced my young family to move to Long Island in pursuit of the American dream. Living through those stresses of life was difficult, but as I look back, I always compare it to my intense army career, in which I survived tough times and in the end became street smart and savvy, enabling me to deal with turbulence. I'll always maintain that my time spent as an army officer prepared me for what was to follow in life.

Richard C. Geschke and Robert A. Toto

Duty, Honor, Country

Yes, there is a band of brothers;
They live among us.
They've heard the sounds of guns,
And as they returned as civilians,
Deep down inside they always remember
Their times of stress and sorrow.
It never goes away,
And at times were camouflaged.
What always remains are the principals
Of Duty, Honor, Country.

Richard C. Geschke
Bristol, Ct
Christmas 2010

CHAPTER 23
TATTOO

In army parlance, life in garrison, such as it was in the zone of Germany, was punctuated by a litany of bugle calls being played out every day. Such calls as "Reveille," "Mess Call," and "Retreat" emanated throughout kasernes in the zone. If you happened to be the officer of the day, it was your responsibility to play the recordings of all the relevant calls of the evening, including "Recall," "Retreat," "Tattoo," and "Taps." I took comfort in making sure these calls were playing over the kaserne loudspeaker system.

To me, the most moving bugle call of the evening was "Tattoo," the second to last call. In the official mandate of bugle calls, "Tattoo" signaled that all lights in the squad rooms be extinguished, and that all loud talking and other disturbances be discontinued within fifteen minutes. The call is wistful and haunting. So this is my "Tattoo" in trying to summarize the last bits of information I have in my duffel bag.

There Were Two Battlefields

Toto and I went to Germany to avoid the war. It wasn't until 1989, when I was watching the news on TV showing the Berlin Wall tumbling down, that the light bulb went off in my head. Hell, Toto and I had spent eighteen months fighting a war without bullets. No sounds of hostile guns had been heard! We had been but mere pawns in the geopolitical climate of the Cold War. This war had been psychological and required the use of intelligence agencies and actual troops on the ground, training under rigorous conditions. We may have been playing war games such as the Warsaw Pact was doing, but make no mistake about it—this was no game.

The name of this policy was called détente, and it was actually propagated by Harry S. Truman, who was essentially the initial Western leader in the Cold War, along with Winston S. Churchill. By the time Toto and I stepped onto the soil of West Germany, America was in its second full generation of continuing the Cold War. Our presence and economic support propped up the European states and helped post–World War II Europe recover fully from the effects of the war. It took two full generations, but without firing one hostile round, the Western Allies won the Cold War, and the guns that were prevalent in the mid-twentieth century were silenced on through the millennium. The celebrations throughout the streets and towns of Europe were even more joyful and pronounced than the celebrations after World War II.

With diplomacy, willpower, and maintenance of a solid mission statement, along with the ability to make changes on the fly and to stick to the plan, victory was possible. What made it even sweeter was that there were no body counts on the battlefield. Funny, no Medals of Honor were handed out in Europe for the Cold War. No Bronze Stars or CIBs (Combat Infantry Badges) were issued! When this victory happened, it was with utmost disbelief and at the same time relief that these hostilities finally were over. We won, no blood. I don't think to this day that the world realizes the concept of finding freedom without the shedding of blood.

During this time frame, another scene was playing out its scenario in the jungles of Southeast Asia. Our commitment in Vietnam emanated from the fifties and continued into the sixties with the support of military advisers. Once Diem was assassinated and Kennedy also met his demise in Dallas, the war was thrown into the hands of Lyndon Baines Johnson. From the false reporting of the Gulf of Tonkin assault until the marines landed in Da Nang, LBJ made a full commitment to Vietnam.

Mind you, there was never any clear "mission statement." The policies used in the defense of our aggressive military posturing in Vietnam emanated from the erroneous "domino theory." This concept stated the following: "If one country falls to communism, its neighboring country will also fall due to the influence of its neighboring Communist." Our mission statement for sending over regular line units in Vietnam was based on false assumptions. From 1965 to 1973, the United States had actively engaged in major combat activities. So in 1971 to 1972, when Toto and I were actively engaged in combat operations to defeat the Communists, we helped propagate the false assumptions of a flawed mission statement, which stated the support of the domino theory. We were wrong all along but too damn headstrong to admit it.

In 1973, all US combat units were deactivated and sent home. The only thing left was MACV (Military Assistance Command Vietnam) advisers to all the active ARVN units. Along the route of the Ia Drang Valley, the North Vietnamese Army struck and continued on to Saigon in 1975 to win the Vietnam War. The regular combat troops of the United States were not there. Ten years earlier, the NVA was stopped in the Ia Drang Valley by the forces of the First Cavalry Division. Without full US forces, South Vietnam was doomed. Never in a million years would the United States have won in Vietnam. In order to win, we would have had to stay there in occupation, not as we did as victors after WWII but as imperial colonialists to continue the war, which in essence would have never ended. Fighting a counterinsurgent war is both expensive and bloody. This was indeed the wrong war at the wrong time at the wrong place. Vietnam was nothing but a huge cesspool in which we as Americans never belonged.

The United States suffered 58,202 KIA (killed in action) during the Vietnam War; 303,704 were wounded. It's bad enough not to be able to win a war, but what makes it worse is that this war had no purpose and no qualified mission statement. The basis and thesis of the war was proven wrong. The domino theory was bogus! All the powers to be were wrong, as pointed out in David Halberstam's classic book *The Best and the Brightest*.

In the time frame after the "Fall of Saigon," our military came to assess the lessons learned in Vietnam. Those professional officers of the Vietnam conflict stated that future conflicts and wars had to bear a clear and concise mission statement that was both realistic and winnable. That generation of Vietnam vet junior officers turned general officers has long been retired.

After the events of 9/11, the United States again entered into a series of conflicts, this time in Iraq and Afghanistan, under the auspices of fighting terrorism. We are fighting the Taliban and al-Qaeda using the same counterinsurgency methods used long ago in Vietnam. Again, regardless of the so-called success of the surge in Iraq, once we leave Iraq, chaos again will rule, as we'll have the "Fall of Bagdad." We have not learned our history lessons. How did we win the Cold War? How did we lose in Vietnam? Here's a factual statement—and please take this as a word to the wise. We won the Cold War without the use of force; we used a superior intelligence scheme along with a proven capitalistic economy, which in the end, was superior to the Communists in Europe. No war in Europe; the guns were silent. However, in Asia, we have fought two wars, and to this day, the Communists are still there. So let's see: We fight wars to eliminate Communists with the force of arms, and they still exist. We fight the Cold War with superior intelligence and a vibrant economy, and we win. Why can't our supposedly superior brains trust and embrace this concept?

Taps

I don't know if it holds true today in our modern army, but in my day, if one entered any officers' club bar, one would always see a sign next to a bell, stating in no uncertain terms that HE WHO WEARS HIS HAT IN HERE BUYS THE BAR A ROUND OF CHEER! The unlucky hat-wearer would hear the ringing of the bell, telling all in attendance that an infraction had occurred. Those were the rules, and more than once, a green second lieutenant would have to buy the house a round of drinks. As my family knows, I always wear my Cleveland Indians hat, and it would be my honor to go into a present-day officers' club and personally ring the bell. The purpose of this action would be to give a toast. My toast would be this: "To all those men and officers who have preceded us in combat, and to all present, it was my privilege to serve!"

GLOSSARY OF TERMS

A

ADA—Air Defense Artillery Branch

AFB—Air force base

AG—Adjutant General's Corps

AFN—Armed Forces Network

AFVN—Armed Forces Vietnam Network

Airborne—soldiers who have graduated from the three-week airborne school conducted at Ft. Benning, Georgia. Airborne school is also called "jump school." Successful graduates earn their "airborne wings."

AK-47—Communist automatic rifle

Ao Dai—traditional Vietnamese dress

APC—armored personnel carrier

Army Brat—son or daughter of a career serviceman

Article 15—non-judicial punishment in the US Armed Forces

ARVN—Army of the Republic of Vietnam

ASP—ammunition supply point

Richard C. Geschke and Robert A. Toto

B

BOQ—bachelor officers' quarters

Brandenburg Gate—monument gate located in East Berlin, gateway to Prussia

Bug Juice—insect repellent

C

CBR—chemical, biological, radiological (warfare)

Charlie—Vietcong

Checkpoint Charlie—checkpoint in Berlin transitioning West Berlin into East Berlin, and vice versa

Chow—a meal

CIB—Combat Infantryman's Badge

Citizen Soldier—non-professional conscript soldier

Class A Uniform—dress uniform

Claymore Mine—command-detonated mine

Click—one kilometer

CO—commanding officer

Cobra gunships—attack helicopters used in Vietnam

Cold War—political, ideological conflict between Western democracy and European Communists

Colors—unit insignia placed on a flag guidon

CONUS—Continental United States

C-Rations—canned ready-to-eat meals

Crossed Rifles—officer's lapel insignia signifying the infantry branch

224

CWO3—chief warrant officer third class

CZ—Canal Zone (Panama)

D

DD-214—Department of Defense separation from service document

DEROS—date eligible for return from overseas

Deuce and a Half—two-and-a-half-ton truck

Didi Mou—Vietnamese for "go away"

D-Mark—Deutsche mark

DMZ—demilitarized zone

Drops—dropping time served in a combat zone

Duty Train—military train traveling between West Germany (zone) to West Berlin, and vice versa

E

E-3—Enlisted Grade 3/Private first class

E-4—Enlisted Grade 4/Specialist 4 or corporal

E-5—Enlisted Grade 5/Specialist 5 or sergeant

E-6—Enlisted Grade 6/Specialist 6 or staff sergeant

E-7—Enlisted Grade 7/Sergeant first class

E-8—Enlisted Grade 8/Master sergeant or first sergeant

EIB—Expert Infantryman's Badge

EOD—explosive ordnance detachment

F

FAC—forward air controller

FDC—fire direction center

Flag Orders—clearance papers to enter Berlin

Flag Shop—Communist political shop

FNG—fucking new guy

Fragging—the practice of killing officers who were disliked by enlisted men in a combat zone

Freedom Bird—plane taking GIs back to the United States of America

FRG—Federal Republic of Germany (West Germany)

FTX—field training exercise

G

G-4—division supply office

Garrison—military installation

GI—government issue/US soldier

GPS—Global Positioning System

Graf—Grafenwoehr

Grunts—infantrymen

H

H&I—harassing and interdictory (artillery fire)

Ho Chi Minh Trail—road from North Vietnam through Laos to South Vietnam

I

IOBC—Infantry Officer Basic Course, Fort Benning, Georgia

J

JAG—Judge Advocate General Corps (Legal Branch)

Jeep—quarter-ton military vehicle

K

Kaserne—US Military installation in West Germany

KD Range—known distance (weapons firing range)

KIA—killed in action

Ku'damm—shortened name for Kurfürstendamm, a main avenue in West Berlin

L

Lebensraum—German word for extended living space

Line Unit—combat unit represented by infantry, armor, or artillery

LST—landing surface tank

LT—lieutenant (pronounced El Tee)

LTC—lieutenant colonel Lifer—career soldier

M

M-1 Rifle—basic WWII weapon of American infantrymen

M-1 Thumb—jamming of thumb when failing to clear in time of chambering a round and being hit by the bolt. Ouch!

M-14 Rifle—basic Cold War weapon of the late 1950s to early 1960s

M-16 Rifle—basic weapon employed by the infantry in Vietnam

M-60 Machine Gun—basic machine gun utilized by the infantry during the Vietnam War

M-60 Tank—basic battle tank utilized during the Cold War and Vietnam War

M113A1 APC—troop-carrying armored personnel carrier utilized in the Cold War and the Vietnam War

MACV—Military Assistance Command Vietnam (American ARVN military advisers)

Marker—navigation course destination

Mekong Delta—southernmost region of Vietnam, mostly swamp tropical vegetation

Mess Hall—army dining facility

Morning Report—military unit's daily attendance report

MOS—military occupational specialty

MP—Military Police

MPC—military payment certificate

N

National Guard—state militia organized under the Department of Defense

NATO—North Atlantic Treaty Organization

NCO—noncommissioned officer

NDP—in Vietnam, referred to as a night defensive perimeter

NVA—North Vietnamese Army

O

O-Club—Officers' Club

OCS—Officer Candidate School

OER—officer efficiency report

Old Man—commander of a unit company grade or higher

Operation Phoenix—clandestine covert assassination operation conducted in South Vietnam

OP—outpost utilized on an NDP for advanced warning in Vietnam

Outpost City—West Berlin

P

Panzer—German tank

Pathfinder—soldiers trained in advanced land navigation and tactical air traffic control. Airborne training is a prerequisite for soldiers attending this school. In the 1960s and 1970s, this school was conducted exclusively at Ft. Benning, Georgia.

Pay officer—major secondary duty of an officer in charge of paying the troops

PBO—army property book officer, asset account manager for army units

PCS—permanent change of station

Pima Equipment—expensive military assets

PIO—Public Information Office

Policed—cleaned up

PPX—Pacific Post Exchange

Profile—medical condition

PX—post exchange (store)

R

R & R—rest and recuperation

Ranger—soldiers who have graduated from the strenuous nine-week combat and military leadership course at Ft. Benning, Georgia.

> *Successful graduates earn their "ranger tabs." Graduates of the winter course have their tabs sewn with white thread.*

Redeye Missile—shoulder-fired heat-seeking missile

REMF—Rear Echelon Mother Fucker

Repo Depot—replacement center

ROTC—Reserve Officer Training Corps

RVN —Republic of Vietnam/South Vietnam

S

S-1—battalion or brigade personnel office

S-4—battalion or brigade supply office

SDS—students for a Democratic Society

Secondary duties—non-primary duties of officers performed periodically, such as "officer of the day"

Secondary Equipment—low-value military equipment

SFC—sergeant first class

Short—less than thirty days left in a combat tour

SKS Rifle—Chinese communist rifle

Slick—UH troop-carrying helicopter

Spooks—intelligence agents

SS Units—German storm troopers

STD—sexually transmitted disease

Supernumerary—superior soldier

Swastika—Nazi crooked cross

T

TO&E—Table of Organization and Equipment

Top—first sergeant

The Turk—in the NFL, the person who delivers the bad news of cutting a player; in the military, it is considered the Grim Reaper of bad news

The wall—wall constructed in East Berlin, separating East Berlin from West Berlin

The world—the United States

TWs—tropical worsteds (Class A uniform)

U

USAREUR—US European Army Command

USO—United Services Organization

V

VFW—Veterans of Foreign Wars, an independent nongovernment organization

Vol Indef—voluntary indefinite commitment of a junior officer for extended duty

Volunteer Army—non-conscript army, all volunteer

Vietcong—South Vietnamese local guerilla troops

Vietnamization—turning over combat responsibilities from the USA to the ARVN

W

Warsaw Pact—Eastern European communistic countries military alliance

West Point—US Military Academy

Wilco—will do

X

XO—executive officer

Z

Zone—West Germany

NOTES

The vast majority of the preceding text recounts the direct experiences of the two authors as they lived through these army tribulations. In some instances actions are attributable to exact dates and times, while in other instances, an approximate time line was established and identified. On more than one occasion did the authors avail themselves of calendars circa 1969–72.

Most of these experiences are indigenous to the authors. However, in the historical perspective of the times, the authors remember the current events of these past times and live them firsthand; therefore, they are able to relate them without the use of reference materials because none were needed. The notes below reference direct quotes of written historical perspectives or were written remembrances used to substantiate the memoirs contained in this book.

page 1 "We Gotta Get Out Of This Place," The Animals, 1965.

page 8 The New Frontier, USGPO, Inaugural addresses of presidents of the United States: George Washington to George W. Bush, published: Washington, DC.

page 8 "We dare not forget…," ibid.

page 8 "Let the word go forth …," ibid.

page 9 "Born in this century …," ibid.

page 9 "and unwilling to witness …," ibid.

page 11 "Hitler's concept of concentration camps …," ibid.

page 12 "I would say to the house …," Winston S. Churchill, *Never Give In!: The Best of Winston Churchill's Speeches,* Hyperion, 206.

page 13 "With malice toward none …," Brian Lamb and Susan Swain, editors, *Abraham Lincoln: Great American Historians on Our Sixteenth President*, C-Span, 2008.

page 14 David Halberstam brought forth, David Halberstam, *The Best and the Brightest*, Ballantine Books, 1993.

page 24 "From Stettin in the Baltic …," Winston S. Churchill, *Never Give In!* Pimlico, 2003.

page 25 A Divided Germany, Winston S. Churchill, *The Second World War, Triumph and Tragedy*, Folio Edition, 2000, 513–522.

page 47 The first artillery round was fired at Grafenwoehr …, www.army-technology.com/projects/grafenwohrarmybase.com.

page 43 The US Army had control of Camp Wildflecken …, www.wildfleckenveterans.com.

page 53 I became enamored …, Winston S. Churchill, *The Second World War, Triumph and Tragedy,* Folio Edition, 2000, 513–522.

page 66 Four Dead in Ohio, James Michener, *Kent State: What Happened and Why*, Random House, 1973.

page 83 To Captain T, I say: Heinrich Heine, *Germany. A Winter's Tale*, Mondial Books, 2007.

page 84 "There is one sign the Soviets can make …," Gerald M. Boyd, "Raze Berlin Wall, Reagan Urges Soviets," *New York Times, June 18, 1987.*

page 118 the dreaded black palm, photograph courtesy of Timothy G. Davis, www.timothygdavis.com.

page 189 Oh, say can you see ..., Francis Key Scott, 1814, www.usa-flag-site.org/song-lyrics/star-spangled-banner.shtml.

page 221 The United States suffered ..., The International World History Project, www.history-world.org, *Vietnam War Statistics*, edited by P. A. Giusepi, "A Letter to the Wall."

All other photographs are from the personal collections of Robert A. Toto, Richard C. Geschke, and Thomas Couch.

ABOUT THE AUTHORS

Richard Geschke is a 1969 ROTC graduate of Kent State University. He lives with his wife in Bristol, Connecticut.

Robert A. Toto is a 1969 ROTC graduate from Northeastern University. He and his wife live in North Attleboro, Massachusetts.

CPSIA information can be obtained at www.ICGtesting.com
Printed in the USA
241247LV00001B/5/P